Advance Praise for Jane Adams's
When Our Grown Kids Disappoint Us

"This book fills a vacuum so wide and deep that even just the title can offer hope to millions of parents who have a desperate need for it! Jane Adams's empathy, understanding, and insight is evident on every page."

—M. Scott Peck, M.D., author of
The Road Less Traveled

"Any parent dealing with difficult or disappointing adult children will feel profoundly understood and comforted by Jane Adams's wise words. Better still, her book offers practical guidance on how, when, and why parents should lovingly but firmly disconnect from their grown kids and reclaim their own lives."

—Judith Viorst, author of
Grown-Up Marriage

"*When Our Grown Children Disappoint Us* is balm to a whole generation of heartsick parents who followed Dr. Spock's edict that we must accept *everything* thrown at us by our beloved offspring so that THEY are happy and secure. Heaven knows we wanted the best for those precious infants born in the fifties, sixties, and seventies— only to be baffled by their inability as adults to get a grip on life. Guilt is the constant companion of aging parents who would like, now, simply to 'have a life.' Ten pages of this wonderful book by Jane Adams will drop your blood pressure 20 points and remind you that it's your turn now. This is, indeed, a *very* important book! It will remind you that you are NOT alone."

—Ann Rule, author of
Every Breath You Take

"Leave it to Jane Adams to make us face up to our deepest family secrets about a common outcome of family life we'd prefer to deny: that sometimes our adult children break our hearts. Read this groundbreaking book about the next phase of baby-boomer parenting, know that you are not alone, and draw comfort from its message—you can find joy and hope in family life even when it doesn't turn out the way you'd hoped it would."

—Pepper Schwartz, Ph.D., author of
Everything You Know About Love and Sex Is Wrong
and Professor of Sociology, University of Washington

"*When Our Grown Kids Disappoint Us* is groundbreaking, courageous, practical, sympathetic, wise, and concise. Jane Adams offers concrete assistance as well as comforting counsel to a large group of parents who are reaching or have reached the end of their rope. This is a superb book, one that should reach a wide and heretofore ignored audience."

—Edward Hallowell, M.D., author of
The Childhood Roots of Adult Happiness
and instructor at the Harvard Medical School

"Dr. Adams's book offers wisdom, comfort, and community to the countless parents whose adult children continue to bind them in ties of guilt. And then she helps them break free."

—Suzanne Levine, author of
Father Courage

"A thoughtful, tough-minded book to help tormented parents let go of their guilt, accept the fact that their kids may not have become who they hoped they would be, and to recognize and value those children for who they really are so they can move forward with their *own* lives—a valuable, important message!"

—Marilyn Nissenson, coauthor,
Friends For Life: Mothers and Their Adult Daughters

"Finally, a book for all those parents who did their best at parenting but found themselves humbled, saddened, and sometimes shocked at the outcome! Jane Adams has written almost the unspeakable—that it is permissible and even advisable for parents of adult children with big problems to get on with their own lives. Adams takes on many themes other authors dare not even touch—like unwieldy guilt, parental narcissism, the never-empty nest, the helping-too-much syndrome, and even forgiveness. Mandatory reading for parents who have suffered from obsessive regretting about parenting—it will serve as a giant dose of group therapy!"

—Dr. Laura Kastner, Ph.D., author of
The Seven-Year Stretch: How the Family Works Together to Grow Through Adolescence and *The Launching Years: Strategies for Parenting from Senior Year to College Life*

"Jane Adams reaches out to parents who are enmeshed in the troubled lives of their adult children, encouraging them to let go with love and discover the well-earned pleasures of postparenthood. The testimonials of her disappointed parents show how the evolution of a whole and separate self can be a lifelong process on both sides of the generation gap."

—Sandy Hotchkiss, author of
Why Is It Always About You?

*f*P

When Our GROWN Kids Disappoint Us

Letting Go of Their Problems,
Loving Them Anyway,
and Getting on with Our Lives

JANE ADAMS, Ph.D.

FREE PRESS

New York London Toronto Sydney Singapore

*f*P

FREE PRESS

A Division of Simon & Schuster Inc.
1230 Avenue of the Americas
New York, NY 10020

FREE PRESS and colophon are
trademarks of Simon & Schuster, Inc.

For information about special discounts for bulk purchases,
please contact Simon & Schuster Special Sales at
1-800-456-6798 or business@simonandschuster.com

Designed by Jan Pisciotta

Manufactured in the United States of America
1 3 5 7 9 10 8 6 4 2

Library of Congress Cataloging-in-Publication Data
Adams, Jane.
When our grown kids disappoint us : letting go of their problems, loving them
anyway, and getting on with our lives / Jane Adams.
p.cm.
Includes index.
1. Parent and adult child. 2. Adult children—Family relationships. I. Title.
HQ755.86. A33 2003
306.874—dc21   2003044830

ISBN 0-7432-3280-1

To Suzanne and Bob Levine, without whom...
and to Jonathan, Sam, Noah, and Jadyn, and their parents

Contents

⌒

When Our
GROWN Kids
Disappoint Us

Introduction

⁓

THIS BOOK IS FOR YOU if your life feels out of control because

- Your adult child can't or won't leave home.
- Your adult child has a problem with drugs or alcohol.
- Your adult child can't get or hold a job.
- Your adult child is chronically depressed.
- Your adult child is excessively dependent.
- Your adult child can't support himself.
- Your adult child has an eating disorder.
- Your adult child is mentally ill or suicidal.
- Your adult child is estranged from friends and family.
- Your adult child is in trouble with the law or lives outside it.

This book is for you if your grown kids' problems have taken over your life. If they're draining you financially, causing stress in your marriage or relationship, affecting your health, interfering with your career, delaying your retirement, isolating you from your friends, creating rifts in your family, threatening your security, or keeping you awake at night.

This is a book about us, not them—about the ordinary disappointments of postparenthood and the extraordinary ones. About expectations that were never very realistic and those that were, given who we were and are and who our kids were and are. Big disappointments and small ones, big heartaches and little worries, expressed by parents whose kids have still not lived up to their potential; who've failed to thrive; who haven't grown up and show few signs of doing it any time soon; who haven't gotten their act together and taken it on the road; who are trapped in the world of abuse and addiction, disabled by mental or physical illness, in trouble with the law or living outside it, enthralled by cults or gurus, enmeshed in abusive relationships, unable to make or keep their commitments, still struggling or already given up.

This book is for you if their problems are getting in the way of your happiness as well as their own and their inability to get their lives started is driving you crazy. Because if they're barely hanging on, chances are you are, too.

May I Talk To You Privately?

As a social psychologist and as a parent, I've been listening to people talk about their children for over 25 years. When *I'm Still Your Mother: How to Get Along with Your Grown-Up Children for the Rest of Your Life* (1994) was published, there were always a few people in the audience when I made a speech or media appearance who took me aside afterward and whispered, "May I talk to you privately?" They wanted advice, information, and support from someone who understood what they were going through—not just the ordinary problems and minor irritants of postparenthood but the fear, worry, resentment, impatience, and frustration of parents whose adult children are failing to thrive.

"Failure to thrive" is how pediatricians describe developmental delay in children who were deprived of nourishment and nurturing at a critical point in their infancy. These days, the term commonly is used by psychologists to characterize delayed adult development in postadolescents—twenty- and even thirty-somethings—who just can't seem to grow up.

Consider these statistics:

- Twenty-eight percent of 21-year-olds have downsized the ambitions they had for themselves at 18, and

50 percent of persons 21 to 30 believe their goals will
never be accomplished.[1]

- Fifty-eight percent of 21- to 24-year-olds live at home
  or have boomeranged back in the last two years; for
  25- to 34-year-olds, the figure is 34 percent.[2]
- Independent adulthood is achieved five to seven
  years later by young adults than it was in 1960.[3]
- Antidepressant use is highest among 21- to 32-year-
  olds.[4]
- Suicide, alcoholism, eating disorders, and depression
  among young adults over 21 have tripled in the last
  two decades.[5]
- The use of heroin and amphetamines among young
  adults has quadrupled in the last five years.[6]
- Forty percent of young adults 18 to 35 are excessively
  dependent on their parents for financial, emotional,
  and physical support.[7]
- Over half the parents of 21- to 32-year-olds contribute
  a quarter or more to the income of their grown children, in money, goods, and services.[8]
- Sexually transmitted diseases, unplanned pregnan-
  cies, and abortions are higher in young adults than
  they are in teenagers.[9]

Of course, statistics are just numbers unless one of
them happens to be your kid. The one who can't or won't

leave home. Who's addicted, dependent, disturbed, or depressed. Who's chronically in debt and counts on you to rescue him. Who's aimless, isolated, and alienated. Who can't face responsibility. Who's just marking time or even doing it.

Behind every one of those statistics there's someone else besides that adult adolescent whose life is falling apart. There's a parent whose heart is breaking, who's crying herself to sleep in the privacy of her bedroom, or scratching his head in confusion, wondering, Where did we go wrong?

Whose Story Is This?

We are a generation of whom much was expected, we boomers, and in turn we expected as much, if not more, of our own children. And while we have spent enough time in the offices of psychiatrists, counselors, and "specialists" to know that their problems and failures are theirs, not ours, we don't believe that for a minute. Or, at least, we're not totally convinced.

"This story is about them, not you," their counselors, therapists, lawyers, and especially their siblings (the ones who are fine, thank God) tell us, and it is. But we have a story, too, and feelings and fears and burdens and beliefs that nobody talks about and only the ones we don't lie to (our partners, our shrinks, and maybe our one closest friend who'd never tell anyone) are able to hear, and respond to, and help with whatever we need, which is sometimes an objective perspective, other times a referral to a professional, but usually just being there and listening.

Here are those stories and here are those feelings, as well as the distillation of all that well-meaning advice and that occasionally insightful explanation. And here, too, are the positive, life-affirming, burden-easing things you can learn from the experiences of hundreds of parents of kids who've let them down.

That sounds like a self-centered way to describe those parents and the choices their kids have made, doesn't it? After all, whose life is it, and who are we to judge how they should live it? Just because they didn't finish school, or marry the right person, or worship the right way, or live the way we do, or make the choices we hoped they'd make, or leave the nest on time, or develop the morals or standards or character we had every right to expect they'd manifest by now, who are we to say they've failed?

Only their parents, for whom coming to terms with our adult children's limitations also means facing our own. Although their names and the details of their lives have been changed, they are as real as you and I, with real kids and real disappointments, and the only reason they told me their stories was that they had to tell someone, and they trusted me to protect their privacy and that of their adult children. So if all you're fuming or frantic about is that he didn't get into Harvard or she's still single at 30, or that their priorities, politics, and partners are different from yours, that's your problem, not theirs, and this book won't help you; count your blessings and give it to someone who needs it.

But if your kid's problems are seriously impacting his or her life and keeping you from reclaiming your own from wherever it was you put it all those years ago, you're at serious risk for failing to thrive yourself, so maybe you'd better hold on to it.

When Bad Things Happen to Good Parents

In midlife, a central aspect of parents' identity is evaluating how our children have turned out; that is, what kind of adults they have become. The lives of our grown children constitute an important lens through which we judge ourselves and our accomplishments; it is through reconsidering their adult successes and failures that we seek, retroactively, to validate the kinds of parents we were and the responsible caring we provided.[10]

As one unhappy parent told me, "When your kids are little, you know what the norms are. You know that even if Jason isn't toilet trained at five, eventually he'll graduate eighth grade without a diaper, and if Jennifer's telling lies at six, by the time she's seven she'll grow out of it. You talk to other parents everywhere from the playground to the pediatrician's office, and you have no shame about sharing the details of your kids' problems because you know they all develop differently, at different ages. But when they're adults, or supposed to be, you feel like whatever's wrong with them is your fault. It's a reflection on how well you did or didn't do your job as a parent. So if they're not doing well—if he's got a drug problem, or if she can't hold a decent job, or if they flunked out of college or are living on welfare or turned out to be selfish or mean or have terrible values or something—you just don't tell anybody else. You're all alone with your worries, and your anger, and especially your disappointment."

It's not a cop-out or even self-serving to say that we were not the only influence in their lives, and their delayed maturity is not the only measure of who we are or even who they are; it's true. Bad things happen to good parents, after all, and vice versa. But the fact remains, as this same parent—a successful, respected woman—told me, "No matter what I've accomplished in my life, if I can't say my kids turned out fine, I will feel like a failure, even if nobody knows it but me."

Our Dirty Little Secret

Here's our dirty little secret—a lot of us are disappointed in our adult children. In the ones who still haven't lived up to their potential, whose lives seem to have come to a full stop just when they ought to be starting, or who've dead-ended down dark or dangerous alleys. And we're not only disappointed—we're ashamed of feeling that way.

We all have our own ways of coping with our secret shame. We console ourselves by whistling in the dark, which helps for a while. We remind ourselves when we hear of some other parent's even greater heartache that *"shana rayna kapora,"* which is Yiddish for "It could have been worse," which usually it could have been. We tell ourselves they'll grow out of it, and in many cases they will. We arm ourselves with the best information, expert assistance, and professional help we can get or afford, which can't hurt and at least gives us the feeling that we're doing everything we possibly can, which we are. Meanwhile, we live one day at a time and focus on the future, which may seem contradictory but in fact is how most of us get by.

The Elephant in the Parlor

What we don't do, though, is talk about the elephant in the parlor. We keep our kids' problems and our pain to ourselves, out of shame, sadness, and self-blame. And that's too bad. Because it helps to talk, to listen, to learn, to share—yes, it really does.

It may be reassuring to learn that you're not alone with your disappointment. To understand why you feel your grown kids' pain so deeply, why you're always in psychic contact with them even though you have no idea where they are, and why it's so hard to know where you end and they begin. To know not just what you can do for them but what you can't.

Because you're not the only parents who feel confused, helpless, deserted, exhausted, useless, guilty, angry, resentful, and worried. Yours isn't the only marriage or relationship that's been stressed, strained, or even sacrificed to your grown kids' problems. You're not the only ones who don't know how to separate yourself from their problems without separating from them. And you're certainly not alone in blaming yourself for your other dirty little secret, which is your envy and resentment of those whose kids turned out just fine.

Frankly, there are some real horror stories in the following pages, and if one of the ways you cope is by telling yourself it could be worse, many of them might be useful in that regard. There are also some hard truths in this book that even your shrink may not tell you—that your expectations are or were way overblown; that it's your narcissism that's the problem, not their choices; that some of it might have been your fault a long time ago but it's too late to change it now; that some kids won't ever grow up or grow out of it; or that even when and if they do, some of the doors you tried so hard to open for them will be shut forever, and, like them, you're just going to have to live with it.

What's taken for granted, though, is that we were all good parents, or at least the best we knew how to be; that we, who were raised to think and feel we were gifted and special, tried to make our kids feel that way, too, even if in some cases that may have been their downfall. It should go without saying that we always loved them, and still do, even if we didn't always like them, and still may not.

What's surprising to some of us is how suddenly and sharply our kids went sideways after they got through what we always thought were the dangerous years of their adolescence without any major hitches. Perhaps the problems that plague them now were always there, but we never knew, and they never told us, and until they were beyond our control or even our reach they seemed to be fine.

Maybe we were in denial, or maybe they were managing okay until the challenges of making a life for themselves overwhelmed them. What we have to do now is not let their challenges overwhelm us.

It may be very difficult to move away from a job that wasn't done perfectly, especially parenting, but parenting skills were never designed to work for grown kids. We need to define the limits of our relationships with them and our involvement in their lives, since those are the only limits we can set now. We need to find ways to stay in meaningful contact with them while we work through our own midlife tasks of coming to terms with our gains and losses, reconsolidating our identity, and reclaiming our lives now that we have reached the limits of our parental role.

Although we have no power to intervene in their lives, we are not entirely helpless. There are some steps and strategies that may nudge them along a bit, and there are things we can stop doing that may be prolonging their dependence and facilitating their failure to thrive.

Remember those times when they were teenagers, and we'd catch a glimpse of the adults they were starting to become, and think, I must have done something right? Most of the people in this book are still waiting for that grown-up to emerge. Some have had their patience rewarded, and others eventually may, because even if their kids screwed up the first act of their lives, we all know F. Scott Fitzgerald was wrong—there are second acts, and third, and fourth, and many of those will have happier endings.

There are opportunities to grow through even the worst of times, to free yourself from the lonely prison of your disappointment in your adult children, which is the only way to free them to grow into the happier, healthier people they still may have it in them to become.

We're all suckers for happy endings and sentimental stories, but there aren't many in these pages because this is an unsentimental book. It's time for us to find our own happy endings, which are waiting to unfold despite—or even because of—what we're going through right now. "You should call this book *Great Investment, Lousy Returns,*" said one parent—a financial planner, by the way. But that only would be appropriate if you believe it's a child's duty to make his parents proud or a parent's obligation to make her children happy. And if these are the only myths this book manages to dispel, you'll get your money's worth.

What sociologists call the "postparental imperative" demands that we make sense of who and what matters when we return to the self we put aside to raise our kids. Because we've done that—whether we think we flunked or passed parenting, it's over. We won't get another chance at it, which is the good as well as the bad news. Our job now is to come to terms with the choices we've made in our own lives, abandon some dreams and commit to fulfilling others, allow the silenced voices inside us to be heard, and make the most of the time that's left. We can do that—we *must* do that—regardless of whether our kids ever achieve what we still believe is their golden, unlimited potential. But that will only be possible if we start concentrating on our own lives while we're waiting for them to get lives of their own.

Chapter 1

~

The Kids Are All Right and Other Lies Parents Tell About Their Grown Children

WE'RE AT DINNER, nine of us, early and late boomers who've cried and laughed together, held and hugged each other through marriages, births, divorces, remarriages, and deaths, the rites and rituals of celebration and mourning that punctuated the beginnings and endings and new beginnings of our lives. We have a history together—housewarmings, promotions, cross-country moves, new careers, the first gray hair, the last great love affair. Mothers and fathers all, veterans of car pools and PTAs and soccer teams, sharing the details of our children's lives the way we always have since those gap-toothed and cowlicked darlings took their tentative steps on the perilous road to adulthood, from her first period to his first learner's permit, through their tumultuous but relatively crisis-free adolescence all the way to the college acceptance letters.

We're over 50 now, and those darlings are in their twenties and even their thirties, and when, as we always do, we ask our peers—the A-list, the nearest and dearest as well as our more casual friends—"How are the kids?" they tell us, as they always do, "The kids are all right."

Except some of us are lying.

Because lots of those kids—our kids, always and forever, even though they've reached their majority by now, are physically fully matured, legally and constitutionally adult and emancipated, and beyond our control if not our concern—are a long way from all right. And we're living with it by ourselves, and we're not telling it to anyone. Sometimes we're not even admitting it to ourselves.

A few of us are just plain telling untruths, some are "editing" or only talking about their other kids who really are okay, others are exaggerating or putting the best spin on the situation, and the rest are simply keeping our mouths shut. Except Lila, because she doesn't have to. Since his infancy, her only child, Peter, has been like the weather report from Honolulu—always fair and sunny. This is a kid who's led a totally charmed life, been a thing of joy and beauty every day of his 24 years, never caused his parents one moment of displeasure or disappointment. And although nothing is certain, so far it doesn't look like he ever will.

Of course there are plenty of Peters out there, great kids who've done their parents proud in any or many ways, who've never caused them any real pain—particularly not the pain of disappointment.

But there are enough others among the population of educated, middle-class 21- to 34-year-olds who started out with all of Peter's constitutional and environmental advantages, including healthy minds and bodies, loving parents, and the potential to become what we all wanted and expected our kids to grow into: independent, generous, kind, happy, successful, law-abiding, contributing members of society who made the most of all the advantages we worked so hard to give them.

Except they didn't.

Between the nine of us there are twenty adult children, and while half are doing just fine (the half we talk about), the other half haven't fared as well. No one picking at the moo shu pork tonight is the parent of a serial killer, but a couple of our kids are in jail, one for fraud and the other for dealing drugs. Some of us know the names of the "best" rehab centers on both coasts and the experts in treating eating disorders or gambling addictions. Others have no idea where in the world our estranged or disappeared adult children are, and every time the phone rings we wonder if it will be the police, calling us to identify their bodies. And one—the one whose final report was a coroner's verdict—will never stop wondering who her bright, funny, promising son might have become if he hadn't hanged himself on his twenty-fifth birthday.

Some of us feel for our friends but privately count ourselves lucky because all our kids' problems aren't quite that awful or final. So he's 27 and still living at home flipping burgers for bozos because he can't hold a better job—in an earlier generation, we tell ourselves bravely, it was common for three or even four generations to live under the same roof. (And maybe we're not crazy about the girl who's living in the basement with him, but at least we know where he is, and his brother is happily married, has a great job and a wife we adore, and is about to give us our first grandchild, so it couldn't be anything we did.)

So she's almost 30 and has had four abortions, one divorce, and a couple of broken engagements, but at least we're still communicating. (And the guy she's going with now has no criminal record; did I tell you her sister is fine, thank you, getting her Ph.D. and going with a very nice guy, and she was the one with dyslexia?)

So he stole the DVD and the TV and the digital camera to sell to pay his dealer, but fortunately it was from us, not from the store, so he didn't get caught, and we responded to the cry for help it so clearly was. (And the psychiatrist says with treatment, the prognosis is good, which is what he said about the other one, and he was right, it was just a stage she was going through.)

So she had a baby by a guy whose last name she didn't even know, but at least she didn't have an abortion and we're thrilled to be raising our grandchild, even though we'd planned to sell the house and buy a condo this year. And he had a child by a girl whose last name we don't even know, but at least we can afford to make the court-ordered support payments he ignores. And he or she is gay, but hey, there's nothing wrong with that, and of course we're marching in the Gay Pride parade next month, even while we're wishing we didn't have to and being glad our parents aren't alive to see it. (And if you think your kid's sexual preference is nothing to be ashamed of or sorry about, you're absolutely right, but that doesn't keep you from wishing it felt better, or that the rest of the world was as accepting as you are.)

For every Peter, there's a Paul or Paula whose parents are unable to take any joy in living because their kids have screwed up or short-circuited the dreams that began the moment the doctor placed them in our arms. Somehow— and none of us is sure exactly when, or why, or even where—our kids took a wrong turn, away from the sunny futures we planned for them and into lives and circumstances we never dreamed of. And while the final grades aren't in yet, it looks like they're flunking Real Life, which can only mean we've flunked Parenting, right? We're just as disappointed in ourselves as we are in them.

The Most Privileged Generation in History— Except Theirs

We were the biggest, richest, most educated generation in history. We reaped the benefit of the economic security that was our parents' most important goal and their gift to us. Even if we put off our own full adulthood a few years longer than the challenges of a depression and world war allowed them to, by the time we were the ages our grown kids are now, we'd internalized our parents' value system. And while we may have rebelled against or ignored those values in our college years, except for the vocal minority who highjacked the culture,[1] we ultimately adopted or adapted them as our own. We not only took advantage of the opportunities our parents provided—we took them for granted, too. We delayed many (but not all) gratifications long enough to earn them; we stayed in our jobs long enough to get a raise, rented until we could afford to buy, drove whatever we had the cash to put down for. And if we tell our grown kids that, which we have a tendency to do, they just groan and add, "Right—and you walked 20 miles in the snow to school, too."

We were eager for our independence, and by the time we had the responsibilities that come with it, we were (mostly) ready for them. We found our place in society and tried to raise our kids with good values, minus the guilt trips our parents laid on us and with a lot more attention to their inner psychological needs than was paid to ours, which partly explains the "Me" decade of the 1970s.

The winds of change were strong enough in those years to blow away the first life structures and relationships some of us had built, creating a culture of divorce as well as 9 million single parents who were raising their children alone by the time the decade ended. Even if our marriages survived the tumult of that time, our attitudes and behavior changed with the sexual revolution, feminism, and the human potential movement. And while most of us knew we were privileged, few of us felt entitled.

At least, not the way our grown children do.

We didn't feel entitled to work that was spiritually fulfilling as well as lucrative; we didn't expect to get both meaning and money out of our jobs.

We didn't feel entitled to achieve our career goals without a long apprenticeship and a lot of hard work; in high school either we were on the college track or the vocational one, which, along with the war in Vietnam, determined which of the those two predictable paths to adulthood arrived with our diplomas or certificates.

We didn't feel entitled to live off our parents, or enjoy the same standard of living at 25 that they didn't attain until years later, or depend on them for what we should have been getting for ourselves. We didn't feel entitled to blame them for our shortcomings or expect them to rescue us time after time from facing the consequences of our actions or dealing with the fallout from our inactions.

Do we sound a little bitter, a little frustrated, even a little jealous of our kids? (That is, when we're not sounding like old fogies, even to ourselves.)

We are, and it's our fault as well as theirs.

Great Expectations: Ours or Theirs?

This is what we expected of the children we raised to be the best and the brightest. "To finish her education, even if it took her a few more years than it took me. To explore what's out there, all the opportunities open to her, and choose one that's likely to give her a rewarding or mean-ingful career, or at least a decent job. To pay her own way, even if I had to provide a safety net for a while. To be emotionally independent—to own her own feelings and not blame me for her failures or need me to con-stantly be shoring up her self-esteem. To play by the rules and not take dumb risks that would ruin her life. And oh, yes, find a cure for cancer, give me a few grand-children, and call home once in a while. Was that too much to ask?"

Carolyn smiles when she says that, in case I don't know that she really didn't expect her daughter to be this generation's Madame Curie, but it's not enough of a smile to crease the crow's feet around her eyes. On a good day she probably looks at least a decade younger than her 55 years, thanks to regular appointments with her colorist and an hour on her exercise bike every morn-ing, but this isn't a good day for her because it wasn't a good one for Lily, her 27-year-old daughter.

Lily just quit the fourth McJob she's had so far this year, and Lily just broke up with her boyfriend, and the Acura that Lily was driving got towed for parking tickets she'd just tossed in the glove compartment, and Lily spaced her appointments with both the career counselor and the shrink, and Lily ran up a $500 long-distance bill because her best friend lives in London and Lily hates to write letters, and Lily never got around to cleaning the house or walking the dog or defrosting something for dinner. Lily didn't even get out of bed until just after noon, and right now she's having one of her migraines.

Before Carolyn even hangs up her coat, she hears all the details of Lily's very bad day, and whatever feelings of accomplishment and satisfaction she felt at the end of her own very long one leach out of her like the last thin rays of sun on this wintry Minnesota afternoon. It was Carolyn's Acura that got towed and Carolyn's phone that's going to be shut off. It's Carolyn's usually immaculate house that Lily and her friends messed up the night before. It was the appointment Carolyn made with a $100-an-hour career counselor that Lily missed and the shrink whose $150-an-hour bills she's paying that Lily forgot to cancel. And it was the dog Lily said was the only thing that ever loved her unconditionally that peed on Carolyn's rug (not to mention chewing up her best Ferragamos and destroying her rose garden) because when Lily moved back in for the third time since she left for college, she brought the dog with her.

"What does that dog have that I don't, besides a smaller bladder?" Carolyn muses ruefully, because if she didn't love Lily unconditionally, she might have said no. No to Lily moving back home, with or without the dog. No to using, and abusing, her car and her phone and her credit cards and all the other things Lily helps herself to without so much as a by-your-leave. She might have let Lily find her own job, instead of finding her daughter a career counselor (who "specializes" in gifted young people like Lily, according to Carolyn), even if Lily had to settle for something a bit less meaningful, lucrative, creative, and fulfilling than she wanted. She might have let Lily worry about her own therapy, especially about paying for it, and find a way to solve her own problems instead of trying to solve them for her. She might even have let Lily—gasp!— be unhappy, if that's what it took to get her to grow up.

Carolyn dropped out of college to marry Lily's father, and when the marriage ended she went to work at an entry-level job in a graphic design firm. She learned how to dress for success in Anne Klein suits she bought on sale and antique jewelry she found at flea markets, which are still her passion. She learned how to impress old clients with her competence and bring new ones in with her flair, how to manage more people and bigger projects, and by the time the firm was bought out by a multinational company, Carolyn was a vice president, and now she's in charge of the entire Midwest division. She didn't get there without learning how to say no, but she can't bring herself to say it to Lily.

Who's in Trouble Here?

Lily's story only differs in the details from the experiences of many of her peers who aren't much farther along the road to self-sufficiency than they were when they were in college, still living at home, still trying to "find" themselves, still unable to start their adult lives, provide for their own basic needs, or make a commitment to anything—a career, a relationship, a goal, a role, a plan. Also like many of her generation, Lily has so much freedom to choose the way her future unfolds that she seems paralyzed by it. She feels pressured to succeed while she's still young, but she missed the last big economic boom and she's waiting to get in on the ground floor of the next one, whenever that happens. She wants to make a difference in the world, but she doesn't think there's anything she can do that will. She's not in serious trouble—yet. But Carolyn is; her fear, anger, and worry about Lily have given her an ulcer.

Carolyn can't be happy unless Lily is, and when she's not fuming about Lily's predicament, she's making excuses for it. Like many divorced women, Carolyn wonders if her own romantic failure is responsible for her daughter's inability to find and sustain a love of her own. She thinks Lily's standards are too high because she's a perfectionist herself; maybe she drove her too hard. She believes Lily's depression may be genetically linked. And it isn't her disappointment in Lily that she dwells on, it's her anger at her daughter for taking so long to get on with her life that she can't get on with her own.

"I get so furious at her sometimes I just have to leave before I lose my temper. A few times I have, and it always ends with both of us in tears and a lot of door slamming. I tell her, Lily, you have your whole life ahead of you, you're healthy and smart and attractive, do something with yourself—anything! Where's your pride, where's your self-esteem? And then for a while she'll get revved up about something, a job, a plan. A few months ago it was acupuncture school in Oregon—now when I mention it, she looks at me like I'm from another planet. But it never works out, whatever it is—there's always some reason why, it's never her fault, and then, boom, she's back here again, watching daytime TV. She's throwing away her life, which makes me mad, because I don't have that luxury; I've got to make the years I've got left count. Some days I look at this kid I spent half my life raising, I gave everything to, I sacrificed so much for, I had such great hopes for, and I think, Why did I bother? And when will it end?"

Not until Carolyn stops worrying about Lily's self-esteem issues, her love life, her career crisis, her living arrangements, her finances, and her depression, none of which she can do anything about and all of which occupy so much of Carolyn's time, drain so much of her energy, and use up so many of her resources that there's not very much left over for her.

It may not end until Carolyn's ready to tell Lily to leave, or at least learn to live within her own means, not her mother's. And it definitely won't end until Carolyn understands that it's Lily's expectations about how her life should be (and what Carolyn and the world owe her) that need adjusting, not her own.

"I think back about what I expected, and maybe it was more than it should have been, but it's not like I pressured her to make my dreams come true. Right now I'd be satisfied if she'd just get a life. If she'd just be happy," adds Carolyn.

Making Them Happy Is Not Up to Us

It must have been easier for our own parents, who didn't worry the way we do about making their kids happy. While none of them wanted us to be unhappy, what mattered more was making sure we had what we needed to assure our own future: good education, an appreciation for hard work, a value of self-sufficiency, an ethic of responsibility.

What distinguishes baby-boom parents from those of earlier generations is how much importance we place on our kids' inner psychological qualities as well as their educational and occupational success, moral and ethical values, and satisfaction in their relationships. A recent study that examined how we evaluate our adult children's achievements and adjustment—and how those assessments affect how we feel about ourselves—indicated that wanting our kids to be personally fulfilled is a goal unique to our generation.[2] Having gone to sometimes extraordinary lengths to ensure it, it's no surprise that our kids grow up expecting us to provide it and give up the responsibility for finding it themselves, in the places that truly adult people discover it: in the satisfactions of work, love, connection, commitment, self-sufficiency, and achievement.

We cannot make our grown kids happy. As long as we expect that we can, they will, too. And we will both be disappointed.

But Can We Be Happy If They're Not?

Very few of us see our children as perfect products. But how we feel about how they've turned out has a great deal to do with our own emotional health. It has significantly positive effects on all aspects of our psychological well-being—our sense of self-acceptance, purpose in life, personal growth, mastery of our environment, and positive relationships with others. It is because parents are pervasively viewed as significant contributors to how their children's lives unfold that the stakes for parental self-evaluation are high; how our kids turn out constitutes powerful statements about our successes or failings as parents. The same study that researched how our assessments of our adult children impact our own satisfaction found that parents who think their children have turned out well have more positive views about themselves and their lives (self-acceptance) as well as a greater sense of meaning and self-direction (purpose in life) than those who don't. Seeing positive "products" of our parenting influences our sense of managing the surrounding world and our general feelings of continued development and self-realization; when our kids are well adjusted socially and personally, our levels of psychological well-being are generally higher and our levels of depression lower. Interestingly, this study found fewer significant linkages between our well-being and our children's educational and occupational achievements, which further supports the conclusion that wanting our kids to be personally fulfilled is a new goal, unique to the baby-boom generation; the data seem to confirm that we are a generation more concerned with their happiness than their success. "Remember how we used to tell them that we didn't care what they did as long as they were happy?" says Jane. "Maybe we really meant it after all!"

If how our kids turn out influences our psychological well-being, it's also possible that our well-being influences how we construe theirs. If we feel good about our lives, we probably see our kids as healthy and happy, proceeding through early adulthood on their own timetable. But if we don't, we focus on their problems and limitations, and see them as the reason we're unhappy, which may help to explain one very surprising finding in this study: Parents who perceived that their children's adjustment was better than theirs was at the same period in their own early adulthood had significantly lower levels of current well-being!

This finding was so counterintuitive to the American Dream—that every generation wants its kids to surpass its own accomplishments—that the researchers could come to only one interpretation of the data: Although parental psychological well-being increases when children exceed even their parents' educational and occupational achievements, parents dissatisfied with their own lives may not reap psychological benefits when they see their children emerge as more self-confident, happy, and interpersonally skilled than they themselves were in young adulthood. In other words, children who are accomplished and well adjusted may occasion pride and even vicarious enjoyment among parents, yet these same wonderful children may also evoke envy and the sense of missed opportunities in some parents' own lives. For children who have not done well, our disappointment and regret may be offset by the lesser challenges they present to our own life accomplishments.[3]

Is this another of our dirty little secrets? Are we jealous of the kids who are living the wonderful lives we always wanted for them?

Ambivalent might be a more accurate description, especially if we're counting up the pluses and minuses in our own lives and coming up short, like Janet, whose husband recently left her for a younger woman. While Janet's pride in her daughter-the-doctor's professional success is wholehearted, she admits to darker, more complex feelings, as well: "Of course I wanted her to do well, and I'm thrilled that she has. But her confidence and self-awareness just stuns me. She's *conscious*, for lack of a better word, in a way I never was. . . . She's so much farther ahead than I was at her age that sometimes I'm almost intimidated by her. There are times I feel a real twinge of envy, not of all that she's accomplished, but of all that she *is*. I think, If I'd been that savvy when I was her age . . . wow, the places I could have gone!"

But that's not the problem facing those whose grown kids haven't realized their dreams, let alone surpassed the ones we had for them. We'd trade our troubles for Janet's in a minute if we could. Meanwhile, as we're waiting for them to do whatever it is they haven't done yet, or stop doing whatever it is that's keeping them locked in a limbo of not quite adulthood, we can comfort ourselves with the knowledge that "turning out" is a continual process, without an explicit starting or stopping point; as long as there's life, there's hope.

It may be difficult to know whether our kids are just going through a stage they'll grow up and grow out of—some day. But if and when they do, or even if they don't, the shape their lives will take and the choices they make are up to them, not us. What's up to us is coming to terms with the choices we've made, and are making, in our own lives. And meanwhile, we're waiting.

Chapter Two

⁓

We're Waiting . . .
and Waiting . . . and Waiting

ALL OVER AMERICA, we're waiting.

Waiting for our kids to move into their own homes and out of ours. To get up before noon or come home before dawn. To start paying their own way and stop expecting us to. To clean up their act, show a little character, take on some responsibility, or take care of the ones they already have. To get free of their demons, get out of their dead-end or destructive relationships, get off the dime or into therapy or out of trouble or back on track. To get their lives together, or at least to stop tearing ours apart.

Our kids aren't kids anymore. They're over 21, and even over 30, and they're supposed to be adults, but even by our admittedly generous standards, they're falling short. So we're waiting.

We're waiting to mellow into the middle of middle age before we're at the end of it. Waiting to do all the things we said we'd do when we were done with braces and baby sitters, learner's permits and college tuitions, summer camps and winter breaks. Waiting to enjoy what we think might be the best years of our lives but we know are the last ones before we have to face up to the inevitability of aging (although so far we've managed to forestall that by a decade or so—60 is this year's 50, 50 is this year's 40, after all).

We're waiting to cut the purse strings, or at least tighten them up. To sell the house and move into an apartment, take a vacation on an island with no telephones, ease out of the rat race and into our prime. To have one last fling with a new love, rediscover our old one, rekindle the romance, and restore the spirit. To retire, regroup, or restart our lives after two decades or more of raising our kids, with whatever resources we've managed to accumulate—not just our pensions and portfolios, our positions and our power, but our other assets as well: our energy, our senses of humor and history, our ability to translate experience into wisdom and maturity, our awareness of time's passing, and our eagerness to make the most of the years of health, strength, and self-sufficiency that are left. (Or at least redefine them as a new kind of older adulthood.)

But in Milwaukee and Muskegon, Newton and Newport Beach, all over the country, we're finding it harder to do all those things than we ever expected because our grown kids aren't doing what we expected of them. They're not letting us get on with our lives because they can't seem to get on with theirs. And we don't know why they can't (although we have our suspicions) or who to blame (besides ourselves) or what to do about it (because we've tried everything, and it's not helping).

In Louisville, Dave and Marilyn are waiting for one son to finish his education and the other to do something—anything—with his. In West Hartford, Cindy and Mark are waiting for Kate to get out of rehab, and in Seattle, Bob and Evelyn are waiting for Larry to get in.

In Boston, Gretchen is waiting for her daughter's eating disorder to get under control, and in Phoenix and New York, Charlotte and Nick are waiting for Shay to leave the cult leader who fathered her children. In Berkeley, Suzanne and Bill are waiting for their son to get out of jail, and in Atlanta, Sylvia and Don are waiting for their daughter to leave the husband who hits her. In Pittsburgh, Paula is waiting for her son to pay his child support so she can see her grandchild; in Schenectady,

Bonita and Ted are waiting for their daughter to leave an ashram in India; and in Los Angeles Lee is waiting for her daughter to come back and get the child she left with her three years ago.

All over the country, we're waiting. And everywhere, we're asking ourselves and each other, *Who knew it would take this long?* and *When will it end?*

When We Were Their Age

Maturity is an uneven process, and the parenting styles of baby boomers fostered certain kinds of maturity as well as deep pockets of immaturity in our children.[1] Our kids had more responsibility for themselves than we did at their age, both because they had to—we weren't home baking cookies, as one of us famously said when her husband was running for president—and because we thought it was good for them. We trusted them to be responsible for themselves while we worked, not only or always at our jobs; some of us were so busy working out our "stuff" that we might not have noticed theirs. "Sometimes I think what happened to him was because I was growing up at the same time he was," says Nan, whose son is in prison. "After my divorce I probably went a little overboard—it was a very different world then than it was when I got married 10 years earlier. I sort of set him adrift while I was trying to find myself, and I might not have given him the attention he needed or modeled emotional stability for him."

According to social philosopher Robert Bly, many parents of our generation taught our children the codes of responsibility, restraint, and renunciation, but we also taught them how to evade the codes. Stepping through the codes was a secret game among parents in the 1970s, a little payback for being a parent.[2] He calls ours a "sibling society" in which many people, our own cohort among them, are making decisions to avoid the difficulties of maturity; even as we hit the magic half-century mark, many of us are still wondering out loud what we're going to be when we're grown up. "We're so busy trying to stay young that maybe our kids have gotten the idea from us that adulthood is nothing worth aiming for," says Beth, who'd be frowning if she hadn't just been Botoxed. "When I was their age, I couldn't wait to be a grown-up. It meant responsibility, but it also meant independence, which is no big deal to our kids. They've been independent in most ways except financially since they were teenagers, with hardly any responsibilities at all."

Prolonging the Search for Identity—
Or Just Avoiding It?

The search for a stable identity is a major challenge of early adulthood. But in a loosely structured society geared to immediate gratification and a culture that encourages self-absorption, the question that epitomizes that search—*Who am I?*—is harder and harder to answer. Uncertain about their goals, career choices, relationships, values, and loyalties, unable to establish a coherent sense of self, many of our grown kids are manifesting identity disorders that are not just temporary adjustments made during late adolescence but permanent maladies that continue through adulthood and are characterized by the inability to make decisions, a sense of inner emptiness and isolation, difficulties with intimacy and relationships, a distorted time perspective, and an acute inability to work.[3]

One explanation for why many kids who seem to have negotiated the adolescent identity crisis successfully evidence symptoms of this disorder a few years later may be that they never really resolved identity matters but simply foreclosed or diffused them. If their choices of goals and values were carried forward from childhood assumptions and identifications and never rethought or questioned during adolescence, what looks to us like failing or giving up—on an initial career choice or a marriage, for instance—may really be the overdue awareness of the fact that they've been living on "automatic pilot" and need to take over the controls themselves.

Some of our kids think marriage might be a shortcut to maturity, as if a ring and a license and monogrammed towels automatically confer adulthood. These "starter marriages," which often break up within the first two years, represent a kind of identity foreclosure in which the principals adopt someone else's beliefs, values, and attitudes instead of achieving an identity through a personal exploration of their own. Marriage may seem an easier path to adulthood than figuring out their own lives; divorce often follows once they realize it may, in fact, make it harder. And sometimes the consequences of this unconscious attempt to establish a self or shore up a shaky one result in responsibilities our kids aren't really ready or able to assume, which is why nearly 3 million of us—at all socioeconomic levels—are primary caregivers to our grandchildren.

In other cases, marriage provides what some of our adult kids who have been floundering through their twenties need to achieve a coherent and stable identity. "We were very concerned about him until he was in his early thirties," says Buddy. "He had no goals and he didn't stick to anything for long. He had a series of jobs with no future and ran through girls like Grant through Richmond. He drank a lot of beer and smoked a lot of dope. Then he met a girl he really loved who told him she didn't want to marry a stoner with no ambition, and he cleaned up his act pretty quick. Now they're buying a house and talking about having a baby." Adds Mary Jo, his wife, "Our other boys came out of college pointed in specific directions, and they got where he is now a good 10 years earlier; I think some men just need to be married in order to start their lives, and he was one of them."

It may be difficult to evaluate whether, when our children marry, they are attempting to foreclose the search for identity or consolidate it, a necessary prerequisite to real intimacy and the establishment of a new family.[4] It's easier to know when they're stuck in a stage of identity diffusion—when they act impulsively and seem to be drifting through life without a sense of coherence or purpose, carefree and irresponsible well past the time (we think) they ought to be settling down. Feeling so uncertain of who they are, so unable to control any aspect of their lives, they react to whatever happens to them rather than actively choosing a direction and moving toward it. They passively allow others to confer an identity on them and define who they are, something that's easy enough to do in a market-driven society that's happy to do it for them, that says we are what we wear, drive, own, buy, or consume.

Identity foreclosures and diffusions are the beginning, not the end, of establishing a core ego identity—of having an answer to the crisis of choosing a self that can answer the question *Who am I?* In the middle of that process is a phase known as the moratorium, a period in which to explore, test, and rework identity possibilities. This period of seeking and grappling, once considered to end by the time young people graduate from college or at least by their early twenties, has lengthened as "youthhood" is increasingly prolonged and maturity harder to attain, especially in the absence of traditional social markers. Adulthood has become a difficult and hazardous journey for many of our children, not a destination of safety and security that is reached once and for all.[5]

Excuse Us, But We're Having an Identity Crisis, Too

One of the reasons it's so hard for us to cope with the identity crises of our "adultolescents" when they're not resolved in what we think is a timely fashion is that we're having our own—or, at least, we would if they'd let us.

The end of what's been called "the parental emergency"[6] stimulates us to reconsider and reconsolidate our own identity, which is one of the most important psychological tasks of midlife.

Despite the physical signs of aging, the acknowledgment of our mortality, and even the narrowing of our options, we're a long way from over, even if we're finally too old to be the youngest anything (president, Nobel Prize winner) or the first woman who (went into space, ran a Fortune 500 company). We're more curious and excited about the next stage of life than we used to think we would be, more aware of its possibilities than focused on its limitations, particularly if we've managed to stay healthy, achieve a reasonable level of financial security and professional fulfillment, and find intimacy and support in sustained and sustaining relationships. And we are more than ready to maximize our personal freedom and minimize our personal responsibilities.

But when we're stuck in a role that can't change because the "emergency" isn't over, we feel out of sync, off time. We envy our peers who've retired from parenting because their job is done, while ours is not. And we can't move into our second adulthood until we're finished with our first—which may not be until they've at least started theirs. "I've been waiting so long for her to be on her own so I can be, too," says Carolyn, a sentiment echoed by all the troubled postparents who are wondering if that day will ever come.

Our Other Unfinished Task

Like Carolyn, we may be using our kids' apparent inability to manage their own lives as our excuse for not letting go when the psychological demands of midlife require us to reconsider our own identity status—to find a new answer to *Who am I?* besides *Parent*—and to finally confront issues of separation and individuation we may not have resolved in our own adolescence that are stimulated by the end of theirs.

Separation is a lifelong process; from infancy on, we are threatened with the loss of those we love and the roles they have occupied in our lives. Individuation—the means by which we distinguish ourselves from others—continues well into our second adulthood; the less we become someone's parent, the more we become someone else, the "other" we also are, which may be a very frightening prospect, particularly if we have neglected our own development while we concentrated on theirs.

Our own early experiences with separation and individuation have the greatest influence on how we deal with separation throughout our lives.[7] If we were abandoned or rejected by our parents during our childhood or if our adolescent separations from them were problematic, we may unconsciously re-create that experience with our kids, or even make them feel so guilty about moving toward independence that they stop seeking it. Each of our children in a different way stirs up throughout his or her development the same conflicts we experienced at the same stage in our own lives, and although consciously we may be trying to help them let go of us, unconsciously we may also be sabotaging their efforts.[8] We will have to come to terms with our own separation anxieties—both as the parents we are and the children we were—in order to let them work through theirs.

Two Kinds of Parents, Same Kind of Kids

Jessie, a self-described "prototypical baby boomer" who went to Woodstock, lived in a commune, followed a rock-and-roll band around the country, and was 31 before she got married, thinks it's hard to know how what you did or didn't do affected who your kids became. "When they were growing up, we were either the kind of parents who were extremely involved in every aspect of their lives, or the kind who let them make their own choices, either because we believed it was the right way to raise them or because we were lazy and it was easier to do it that way. Either you pushed your kids to be superachievers and organized every minute of their lives or you encouraged them to express their own individuality by letting them do those things themselves, pretty much on their own timetable, figuring that at some point their motivation would come from inside, not outside—not from our nagging or demanding. But it doesn't seem to have made any difference; both kinds of parents are having problems with their grown kids. My best friend was one of those superorganized parents who pushed her kids to excel, and one of them's a drug addict. And I sort of let mine make their own rules and do their own thing, and so is one of them."

That's a consolation to Jessie when she falls into blaming herself for her daughter's problems. "Maybe as a parent I didn't pay enough of the right kind of attention at the right time in Megan's life. But Alexa did, and we're both in the same boat. So what does that tell you? That it doesn't matter? That there's no connection to how you raised them and how they turned out? How can that be?"

We hold on to the belief that how our kids turn out is determined by the kind of parents we were because without such predictability, we would be lost. Certainly the influence of parents is great—but if it were all, none of us would find ourselves in our present predicament, because even if we didn't do all the "right" things, we certainly didn't do all the "wrong" ones; we didn't abandon them or beat them or starve them or tell them they were worthless or lazy or stupid.

While common sense tells us there is a connection between how children are raised and what kind of adults they become, it's not clear how influential child-raising techniques are compared to other factors such as heredity, inborn personality traits, the "fit" between parent and child, the influence of peers and that of the culture and environment.

It's widely if erroneously believed that the so-called permissive parenting espoused by Dr. Spock led to our own generation's failings—that we were spoiled and indulged and therefore disrespectful of our institutions and dismissive of our elders. It's easy enough to assume that a child raised with no limits on his or her behavior might have difficulty adjusting to a world that demands some self-discipline, but it is just as easy to assume that that child might welcome, even crave, such limits, and impose them on him- or herself.

Authoritative, authoritarian, or permissive, even those of us who helped them with their homework every night, schlepped them to lessons and practices and enrichment activities, scheduled every minute of their spare time and were very involved in their college planning heaved a big sigh of relief after it was over. Having gotten them this far, though, a surprising number of us stepped back and left their education and training after that to them. Mindful of the ambitions our parents had for us, and the sometimes heavy-handed way they tried to persuade us in what they thought were the right directions, we resolved to let our children make up their own minds about their future. Scared off as colleges moved from acting in loco parentis to a new role mandated by federal legislation that erected a wall between parents and university administrators and relegated us to onlookers in our kids' education who weren't even allowed to see their grades unless they gave permission, many of us abdicated any responsibility to help them choose their courses, plan and prepare for their future, or draw any meaningful connections between their educational credentials and future career opportunities; that was the job of their college advisers. Consequently, many of our kids emerged from the protective shelter and structure of higher education with misaligned ambitions that weren't connected in any realistic way to a specific career path. Since there were more of them who expected to be professionals than there were professional jobs to be had,[9] it was a rude awakening, for us as well as for them.

In Whose Good Time?

Maturity and independence didn't necessarily arrive with their college diplomas. We assumed they would, because we remember it happening that way for us (regardless of whether it actually did). We didn't and still may not recognize the vastly changed reality they graduated into. It turned out that leaving college did not, after all, mean they didn't need our emotional and financial help, then and for a few years thereafter.

Some of us weren't troubled by that—at least, not immediately. If we could afford to, we subsidized graduate school or travel or "interesting experiences" or even just hanging out—the extended moratorium that allowed them to dawdle a little before they "got serious" about their lives. We assumed that in good time they would. But "good time" has been arriving later and later for some of them, particularly those whose immaturity is characterized by partially formed skills, ideals, and identities. That description fits Mac's grown son all too well: "He only has jobs that are easy to get and easy to quit, that don't ask much of him or require any real effort to master. If they do, there's always something wrong with them—they're ruining the environment or exploiting the worker or hampering his creativity. They pay him enough money to live on, but just barely; my wife is always slipping him a little extra when he comes to visit, which she thinks I don't know, and sending him home with whatever's in our freezer. If she had her way, he'd still be bringing his laundry home! I thought by the time he was a year or two out of college he'd find something he wanted to do, focus on his goals, be responsible for himself financially, and start acting like a grown-up. But he's almost 30, and he still hasn't. He lives on the margins of society—at least, the kind of society we raised him to be part of. He's not exactly a bum, but I wouldn't say he's thriving, either. He's not who I thought he'd be, that's for sure."

Addicted, Depressed, and Dependent: A Detour or a Final Destination?

Some of our kids, even those who got off to what seemed like a promising and timely start, found life as an adult overwhelming. It was harder and less rewarding and lonelier and certainly less fun than it had looked, so they regressed and retreated, existing in a space that seems to have opened up between adolescence and adulthood, unable or unwilling to leave it. Along with their increased sense of entitlement has come an increased sense of being disenfranchised in a world that doesn't seem to care whether they grow up or know what to do with them when they do.

The kids we worry most about—as distinguished from those who merely exhaust and exasperate us—haven't just stalled, faltered, failed, burned out early or lost valuable ground in the establishment of a workable life structure. They're depressed, dependent, and dispirited, afraid, unable, or uninterested in going forward with their lives. Or they've detoured into drugs and alcohol, destructive relationships, and diminished possibilities, in what looks to us like an irreversible downward spiral.

So we are frustrated at best and frightened at worst. We feel cheated by their inability to realize their potential. And even though we know we didn't make the same mistakes with them we think our parents made with us, that doesn't seem to have had much to do with how they turned out, which has at least one unexpected benefit: We may (finally) stop blaming our parents for how we did.

Parenting is a chancy business, composed of many things we can't control, including luck. Although we know that adulthood means taking responsibility for one's life and facing the consequences of one's actions, it's sometimes very difficult to let our grown kids do that. In the first few years of their adulthood, it's not uncommon for us to give in to the tendency to make their problems our problems, to solve them for them, if we can, rather than let them (and us) suffer through the painful process of trial and error. What's even harder is accepting the possibility that we did something wrong, that we failed them—and then detaching ourselves from the outcome of our parenting and refusing to let it ruin the rest of our lives.

Chapter Three

Whose Fault Is It, Anyway?

It was because I worked outside the home.
It was because of the divorce.
It was because we gave them too much.
It was because we didn't give them enough.
It was because we weren't strict enough.
It was because we were too strict.
It was because we set a bad example.
It was because we did something wrong.

This litany of our sins, of commission or omission, intentional or accidental, real or imagined, could go on and on and on—the "coulda-woulda-shouldas." Somewhere there may be parents who don't blame themselves—a little or a lot—for why their grown kids are in trouble. But I've yet to meet them, and if I did I probably wouldn't believe them. Guilt, after all, is the natural condition of parenthood.

Guilt wards off our underlying feelings of grief for our losses and disappointments. Guilt ensures that we continue to suffer, because of course we must. Guilt keeps us from forgiving ourselves, because how can we?

Guilt makes it a story about us, not our kids. Guilt makes us not only responsible but also powerful. Powerful enough to have caused the state they're in, and maybe—if we only knew how—powerful enough to fix it.

But we weren't then and we're not now.

The Two Myths of Parenthood

Both guilty and innocent parents feel guilt, which is nourished by the two myths of parenthood. One myth that most of us believe is that there was a magic formula that could protect our kids from the kinds of problems they're having or the trouble they're in and we didn't know it. The other myth is that there's such a thing as "myfault insurance," and we let the policy lapse when they grew up—if they grew up.

Neither, of course, is true; that's why they're myths. But no matter who tells us that, we don't really believe it.

Self-reproach, self-blame, and a steady supply of guilt are how we respond to our grown kids' failures, foibles, and difficulties. As one writer noted, discussing her daughter's rocky, rebellious, and ruinous adolescence, "She's a bad girl, and I made her. If a factory is judged by its products, I'm a bad mother."[1]

Here are some of the things we blame ourselves for:

- Straying from, rebelling against, or abandoning the values with which we were raised
- Not giving our kids a religious upbringing
- Being too libertarian or permissive in our parenting
- Projecting our expectations onto them
- Spoiling or indulging them for too long
- Depriving them of a two-parent family
- Letting them grow up too soon
- Keeping them innocent too long
- Expecting too much from them
- Not expecting enough of them
- Being too focused on us to pay attention to them
- Needing them to fill up the emptiness inside us
- Overcompensating for what we weren't able to provide for them
- Giving to them out of our needs, not theirs
- Overparenting them
- Underparenting them

The fact is, at one time or another, we may have done—or undone—some or all of those things. But that does not mean either that our actions caused their difficulties or that, even if they did, we can do much about it now.

"I'll Never Make the Mistakes My Parents Made"

At some time, all parents feel guilty about the mistakes we made in raising our children. Sometimes that guilt may even be deserved; the hard truth is that there are some family histories that can't be rewritten or erased. While there are some things for which the words "I'm sorry" may never be enough—child abuse, neglect, failure to protect, our own problems with drugs or alcohol—the more resilient among our kids, especially those who were able to attract the invested regard of others to make up for our lapses, often manage their adult lives well despite the difficult conditions of their childhood. But usually, the guilt and blame are all out of proportion—in our minds or theirs—to the parenting mistakes all of us made.

"I used to say, I'll never made the mistakes my mother made. And I didn't. I just made other ones." I heard that over and over again as I talked to parents.

Those whose grown kids are doing just fine say it, just like those whose kids aren't. And while we might be able to recall our parents' mistakes, bring up every narcissistic injury we suffered at their hands, and distinguish ourselves from them by having done exactly the opposite, we are not exactly sure what our own mistakes were. We feel guilty, but we're not sure why; we blame ourselves, but we're not sure what for; we take responsibility, even ownership of our kids' problems and failures when they rightfully belong to them.

Wrestling Guilt to the Ground

Occasionally our troubled kids are ready to absolve us of blame or guilt even before we are. "It's not your fault," said Heather, hugging her mother, Andrea, when she signed herself into a rehab program. "I don't know what's going to happen to me here. I'm really scared of what I might find out about myself. But I promise you, I had a happy childhood and I always knew you loved me. It's not your fault." But Heather's understanding of Andrea's guilt is rare. More often, guilt, blame, and responsibility are heaped on us by our kids, who know better than anyone how to push our buttons, where we're most vulnerable, and how easy it is to manipulate us into believing that their unhappiness, their pain, their disappointment in a world that hasn't lived up to their expectations, that hasn't noticed (or cared) how special they are, is our fault. If they succeed, they're off the hook; if we take responsibility for how their lives have turned out, they don't have to. And as long as we do, they won't.

When I read Anne Roiphe's description of her journey to understand the roots of the problems that plagued her older daughter, who was addicted to heroin and alcohol and has tested positive for HIV, it had a particular resonance for me. "I struggled for a long time with guilt," she wrote. "I have just about wrestled it to the ground."[2] Noting that her daughter's father was also an alcoholic, she "clung to the image of genetic programming as if it were a life raft that would keep me afloat in a sea of guilt."

Back in the 1950s when mothers were considered to be the cause of all their children's emotional problems, my sister had what was then referred to as "a nervous breakdown." It was 12 years before she was properly diagnosed with bipolar disease, but by that time my mother had eaten herself alive with guilt and turned into an alcoholic. She thought—no, she *knew*—that she had made my sister crazy. Until she died—years after the genetic links to many mental illnesses that often present in young adulthood, like bipolar disease and schizophrenia, had been demonstrated—she never let herself off the hook. And neither has Roiphe, at least entirely. "Genes provide an excuse," she writes, "a kind of half-assed alibi, but they . . . aren't the whole story." Ultimately, she concludes, in a kind of mantra, a prayer to mitigate the guilt she hasn't wholly wrestled to the ground, "I am not responsible. I am not *alone* responsible" (emphasis added).

The Echo of Our Childhoods

Gretchen, who never did anything she couldn't do in high heels, ran the Boston Marathon for the first time last year—on her sixtieth birthday. "To take my mind off things," she says, referring to her 27-year-old daughter's eating disorder, something she is still struggling to understand. Although she was determined not to repeat what she believes were her demanding, narcissistic mother's mistakes, much that Gretchen has read about Abby's disease—and what Abby herself, after a year in therapy, incessantly reminds her—reinforces her feeling that it is somehow her fault. "They say anorexia is a response to feeling powerless when you were a child, which is why you need control so much you'll starve yourself to get it. It usually happens to girls who have overcontrolling, narcissistic mothers or fathers," she muses. "I didn't think I was a narcissist, too, but maybe I was. I guess it runs in the family."

Some sociologists point out that each successive cohort since the Second World War has been brought up by and composed of an increasing number of narcissistic parents, thereby reinforcing the sense of entitlement believed by many to be at the root of our kids' problems. The belief in their own uniqueness and specialness that we encouraged also contributed to their often-unreasonable expectations of especially favorable treatment or automatic compliance with their wishes. And our generation's style of child raising, which tended to be permissive rather than authoritative, reinforced those expectations and that sense of entitlement.[3] "Is it narcissistic to want your kids to be people who reflect well on you?" wonders Peggy, whose children do. "If it is, then you can call me a narcissist." Adds Cleo, "Aren't we all? And haven't we all raised another generation just like us?"

Well, maybe. A certain amount of narcissism isn't only healthy—it's necessary for sustained, realistic self-regard and mature aspirations and ideals as well as for the capacity to feel empathy and love others. While narcissism may, in fact, be a very useful attribute in a culture as concerned as ours is with "impression management," its unhealthy aspects involve an inordinate need to be loved and admired by others that feeds a grandiose and inflated sense of one's own worth; while being skilled in the presentation of self can be a shortcut to success, it may also contribute to a pervasive sense of emptiness.

Gretchen's description of narcissism as something that runs in the family may be accurate; the ways in which we are different from our parents are significant, but those in which we are the same are even more important, although less often recognized and even less often acknowledged. Gretchen's comment that "The day Abby graduated from Harvard—magna cum laude, by the way—I said to my mother, 'See? I turned out to be a good mother after all'" underscores the need some of us feel for our kids to succeed so we can tell a voice in our past—usually a mother—that we were good enough. But Abby's disease has turned the pleasure Gretchen feels in her daughter's other accomplishments into a harsh rebuke, proof that she failed her daughter because she didn't provide her with a steady stream of unconditional love.

Regret Is Guilt Without the Neurosis

While unconditional love may be the gold standard, it's not one most parents are consistently able to meet. The truth is, there are all kinds of conditions surrounding our feelings of love for our kids, not the least of which is their ability to fulfill our dreams of being a perfect parent. "Unconditional love is what you get from grandparents," says Jane. "All my grandchildren have to do to earn it is just *be*. My kids had to do a lot more."

Many of our motives in child raising were not pure. We may have needed our children to meet our own unmet needs and compensate for our own childhood experiences. But that was then and this is now, and all our willingness to take responsibility for their problems cannot fix them, only absolve our kids of the opportunity to do so themselves.

We all know the myth of Narcissus, who fell in love with his own reflection. In books like Alice Miller's *The Drama of the Gifted Child* (originally published as *Prisoners of Childhood*), and in the personal growth and "therapy" culture to which some baby boomers turned for an explanation for our own feelings of inadequacy, we found what we thought was the reason: our parents' narcissism. It was an all-purpose explanation that seemed to fit our experience of having to "earn" our parents' love by gratifying their emotional needs. As the experts on anorexia Gretchen consulted have tried to convince her, there is a significant body of research indicating that parental narcissism is not the only or even the major cause of eating disorders. Certainly a culture that worships slenderness and considers fat a sign of character deficiency is also a factor; Abby's obsession with being thin occurred after she moved to Los Angeles, where a woman over a size 10, even one with a strong sense of self-esteem, often feels like the circus fat lady. But Gretchen isn't having any of it. "It's my fault," she says flatly, and Abby—perhaps in an attempt to get the last word herself—is glad to confirm it. Her alacrity in pinning the blame on Gretchen brings to mind the other figure in that much-maligned myth—Echo, whose power to speak first was taken away by Juno as punishment for having cheated the goddess out of the chance to catch her husband dallying among the nymphs. Unable to win Narcissus' love because she could not speak to him, merely repeat his words, Echo's "form faded with grief, till at last all her flesh shrank away."[4]

Often young people who turn to therapy to make sense of a difficult and confusing time in their lives blame their parents for what has turned into an unexpectedly rocky road to adulthood. Accepting blame as fully as Gretchen does will not make it easier for Abby to get well, only trap her in emotional dependency, which may be as significant a factor in her eating disorder as anything her mother did or didn't do; for all that we venerate it, unconditional love is not an easy thing to live up to. "Nobody will ever love you as much as I do," we tell our children, and for some of them it becomes a self-fulfilling prophecy.

Obsessing over our guilt, real or imaginary, won't help our kids as much as acknowledging that we may not have been perfect parents and allowing ourselves to feel regret that we were not. Nor must we own their sometimes negative assessment of us; it's their story, they're sticking to it, and our only legitimate response is accepting that it is true *for them.* Regret, which is guilt without the neurosis, enables us as well as them to move forward instead of back.

Why Wasn't I Listening?

If our grown kids' problems just seem like an extension of those that have been plaguing them—and us—since adolescence, or even before that, we may be more prepared to consider other explanations besides our own shortcomings as parents for theirs. And if we are, we are several steps ahead of other parents who are taken by surprise when their confident, competent kids manifest symptoms of severe distress. Anxious to find a reason—any reason—for what happened to them, such parents berate themselves for not listening, noticing, or paying attention to "warning" signs.

In many cases, there weren't any: "The first time I knew she had a problem was when she asked me if I'd help her pay for rehab. I said, 'Rehab for what?' And when she said, 'I'm addicted to heroin,' I was completely stunned," says Andrea. "I had absolutely no clue that she was in trouble—her life seemed to be going wonderfully. I thought, This is somebody else's world I've stumbled into, not my daughter's.

"It was very hard to face the reality that there was a lot about my daughter I didn't know," says Andrea. "She kept saying, 'I'm not who you think I am, I'm not your idealized image of me. I can't live up to that any-more, and if you can't let go of it, there's no sense even talking.'"

For a long time, Andrea replayed every moment of Heather's childhood and adolescence, looking for the clue she thought she'd missed, believing it could solve a mystery that baffled her. "I'd say, 'What did I do, I must have done something,' and she'd say, 'Stop it, Mom, don't make it about you, it's about me.' Once I really heard that—and it took a long time!—I was able to stop feeling responsible. That was probably the first step in my recovery: letting myself off the hook."

Even if, like other parents whose grown kids suddenly veer off from lives that seemed to be progressing nor-mally, Andrea could trace the cause of Heather's addiction to something that did—or didn't—happen much earlier in her daughter's life, she might still have been powerless to prevent it. We are not the sole determinants of how our children turn out, after all; it is grandiose and ultimately self-defeating to think that we are.

Heather has been drug-free for three years now—"But who's counting?" asks Andrea with a rueful smile. "Since she wouldn't let me take the blame for her addiction, I can't take credit for her recovery, either. I hope she won't relapse, but if she does, I know it won't be my fault. I couldn't have said that three years ago. I spent enough time in therapy to understand that I was afraid that if I let go of her problem, I'd be letting go of her, too. But it's only because I was finally able to do that—to let her recovery be her business, not mine—that we could continue to have a close, loving relationship."

When the Writing's on the Wall

In other cases—the majority, as a matter of fact—the distress signals were there all along. "He needed attention since he was born, even the wrong kind," says Suzanne of her youngest son, now 30, who's due to be released from prison soon after serving three years of a three-to-five sentence for trafficking in stolen property—computer parts he tried to sell to an undercover cop. "Of course, he told us he didn't know they were stolen, but how can you believe a kid who's been lying to you all his life?" asks her husband, Bill. "He could never tell a straight story; even if you caught him red-handed, he'd look you in the face and swear that black was white." Suzanne, sadly, agrees. "You want to believe them—God, you want to. But enough times they turn out to be lying, and you know you just can't."

Josh's young adulthood, like his adolescence, has been a constant source of misery and disappointment for his parents, who can't understand why the values they modeled, the respect for other people and their property they tried to teach him, failed to "take." Sitting in the backyard of their lovingly restored Craftsman-style house in the Berkeley "flats" amid a profusion of brilliantly orange poppies and sweetly scented lemon magnolia trees, Suzanne, a landscape designer, and her husband, a college professor, look a great deal older than they are and sound as defeated as they felt at the end of Josh's trial on the charges that culminated in a prison sentence.

It wasn't his first run-in with the law. "When he was 14, he was picked up for joyriding—stealing a neighbor's car," Bill recounts. "He said it wasn't his fault, he just went along with his friend. We got him a lawyer and he wasn't charged. Then he started breaking into houses in the neighborhood—not stealing anything, just breaking in." He turns to his wife. "Is that when we got him the psychologist?" She nods. "We couldn't keep him out of juvvie that time. The doctor said, 'Don't try, he needs to learn the consequences of his actions.'"

For a while, that goal seemed accomplished; Josh finished high school and entered college. "I noticed he was wearing a very expensive watch when he came home at Christmas his freshman year," Suzanne says. "I didn't confront him about it—I knew he'd lie to me, and frankly, I just didn't want to hear it."

Arrested later that year for stealing equipment from the college athletic department, he was sentenced to six months in the county jail, despite the best efforts of the lawyer his parents hired to defend him. "We thought, If anything can teach him a lesson, this will," Bill said. "Obviously, it didn't. But that stupid business with the computer chips that got him a prison sentence—that was the final straw. We've paid our last lawyer's bill for him."

Enough years of bailing their son out of trouble of his own making have shown his parents the futility of continuing to rescue him. They have tried, with some success, to set themselves free of feeling responsible for his failures. "We may be disappointed, but we're not responsible," Bill says firmly. And Suzanne adds, "I wish he wasn't where he is. Visiting him is incredibly painful—even in the clothes they make him wear, he seems so out of place there. The only good thing is that at least I know where he is. I'm not waiting for the phone to ring, telling me he's in trouble again. He still has a chance to turn his life around even though I don't think anything we can do will make any difference. He has to make that choice himself. But even if he doesn't, he's still our son. We will never turn our back on him."

Good Enough Is the Best We Can Do

As parents we are fallible beings, sometimes ambivalent about our ability or even desire to put our children's welfare above our own. The "good-enough mother" (of whom British psychologist Donald Winnicott wrote) teaches her child that she is not omnipotent by her manageable and necessary failures to anticipate his every wish and need. By empathizing with and containing or holding his frustration, she enables him to face the frustrations and losses that will inevitably follow, that are part of every life.[5]

Most of us were good-enough parents, which does not stop us from going over and over what we did and what we didn't do, what we might have and what we should have. We seize on the memory of a specific event as if it held the clue to everything bad that followed: "The time I yelled at her when she was three, the time I shouted, 'If you don't stop that I'm going away and I'm never coming back,'" says Gretchen. "That was when her troubles began." "When we got him a lawyer who got him off the first time—if he'd had to face the consequences then, maybe he would have learned his lesson," says Suzanne.

Stuck in guilt and self-blame, we can't accept and grieve our losses or free our children from the burden of our disappointments. Second-guessing the past, we forget how limited our responsibility is for their present. By staying mired in "then," we avoid living in "now." But now is the only time we can make any difference—if not in their lives, at least in our own.

Chapter Four

~

They're Ba-a-a-ck!

THE REVELATION THAT LIFE isn't easy, that many of the trials of the twenties end in errors—in jobs, relationships, living arrangements—comes as an unpleasant surprise and a disappointment to many of our adult children; after all, few of us taught them about failure. Believing that the choices they make now will solely determine who and what they become, feeling that they are about to gamble on their lives, they're stalled, confused, and helpless. Like Lily, they're having what's been called a "quarterlife crisis"—a response to overwhelming instability, constant change, too many choices, and a panicked sense of helplessness.[1] Their search for meaning and fulfillment is marked by apprehension, procrastination, depression, denial, and especially dependence.

The Never-Empty Nest

The phenomenon of the never-empty nest is so unremarkable these days that it almost seems that nothing has changed in the last half century, especially to the Silent Generation born just before and during the war, who remember how common it once was for young adults to live with their parents; even after marriage, couples remained in the family home while they saved for a down payment on one of their own. They moved to the suburbs in the 1950s to raise us, but once they had, we couldn't wait to get out and set up homes of our own.

Usually those first homes or apartments were shared with as many roommates as it took to make the monthly rent. But what they lacked in privacy and creature comforts was more than offset by what they offered: independence. And whether as adults with kids of our own we stayed in the cities or came back to the suburbs for the same reason our parents had, we assumed that when our children grew up, they'd follow our example.

But they haven't. They may be grown up now, but a lot of them haven't left home. And many of those who have have come back, left, and returned again, often a number of times.

There are plenty of reasons for this, as any young adult, his or her parents, and social scientists, demographers, and economists can reel off. It's an unstable job market, with fewer professional, management-track or creative career slots than there are high-aspiring, college-educated young adults who want them. Housing costs have skyrocketed, and our kids have grown used to a higher standard of living than most of them can afford. Sexual freedom is no big deal when you've always had it. Relationships between our generation and theirs are generally closer and more equal than ours were with our parents; as a psychologist specializing in a relatively new field called "emerging adulthood" says, "These young people genuinely like and respect their parents."[2] And independence isn't all it's cracked up to be, especially if your initial experience of the adult world beyond your family's shelter and protection didn't live up to your expectations.

Moving back and forth between the family hearth and a more or less independent life beyond it is a process that is similar in many ways to what occurs in early childhood—the aspects of the "practicing" phases of separation and individuation psychologist Margaret Mahler described as hatching, and refueling.[3] Sometimes coming home is a temporary respite when jobs, relationships, and living situations change. Other times it's furthering a goal both generations agree on; most of us are willing to provide relatively high levels of support if our kids are using that support to better their life chances[4] or doing something we approve of: Says Jeanette, whose daughter has a worthy but poorly paid job in the nonprofit sector, "Housing in this city is out of the question for anyone earning what she does. And what she's doing is important to society. Those are the values we raised her with, and we're proud of her for following them; if living with us is the only way she can do it, then so be it. Besides, she's really nice to have around. We get along much better now than we used to."

The impact on us of having them home is mediated in part by our expectations for their development, which color how we feel about their return to the nest. Since our experiences at midlife are tied to our children's life course, even after they've left home, their transitions confront us with decisions about how much support we can and should give them, financially and emotionally. Refilling the nest represents only one form of support, but it's the one with the most drastic implications for our daily lives.

Whether home is just a pit stop on the road to full adulthood or a haven when role transitions have failed determines how we feel about having them back. In cases where kids return so they can afford further education, or save for a home of their own, or even help us care for their grandparents, it may signal the development of greater autonomy rather than renewed dependence, which will make our experiences with them more positive, if not less conflictual; recent studies indicate that three-quarters of parents report open disagreement with grown kids living at home, most frequently about household help, money, and getting along with other family members, though drinking and drug use, late hours, friends, and work are also perennial areas of disagreement.[5]

Launching and empty nesting play out over many more years than they used to; it's simply a fact of life in the twenty-first century, not an admission of failure—ours or theirs. But in more than a few cases, grown kids come home or never really leave because they can't control the impulse to remain attached. The anxiety that attends the separation process ordinarily accomplished by the end of adolescence paralyzes them, and the result is their prolonged dependence on us. It shouldn't surprise us that after their sometimes-unsuccessful forays into adulthood they come home for succor, sympathy, and support; few of us have given them any reason not to expect to receive it. What does surprise us is that once back, they're in no hurry to leave. And from their point of view, why should they?

It's certainly not because they're the only ones they know who are living with their parents well into their twenties or even their thirties. Leaving home is no longer a single event for a majority of them. Forty percent of young women and 50 percent of young men who do leave home after finishing their undergraduate education subsequently return one or more times. It may take 10 years before they fully shift their home base from under our roof to under their own. And it's the conflict between our realities and needs during that time and theirs that leaves so many of us frustrated, exhausted, and exasperated.

Out of Time and Out of Patience

Like Lily's mother and many parents like her, Sherry is running out of patience. Her 28-year-old son has already boomeranged back home four times, and she can tell it's only a matter of time before he does it again.

Sam moved out of his parents' tree-shaded split-level house on a street full of well-kept homes in a Houston suburb after college. "We went to see his first apartment right after he moved in," says Sherry, a short, plump woman with curly black hair and bright red lipstick who's on vacation this week from the private school where she teaches Spanish and French and where Sam and his older sister Judy (who's a lawyer in Dallas, by the way, and doing just fine) received the kind of education his family couldn't have afforded any other way: it's why Sherry took the job. "Give them a good start and they'll go the rest of the way on their own—that was our plan, anyway."

She remembers when they visited Sam at that first apartment. "You're always leaving your kids some-where—kindergarten, camp, college. You have those contradictory feelings of 'Whew, what a relief' and 'Oh God, I'll miss him.' On the way home, after lining his shelves and uncrating his furniture, Art said to me, 'This time we're really letting go,' and we were both very happy. I said, 'I guess we passed parenting, didn't we?' and he said, 'I think we got an A.'"

"And then, just about the time you stop patting your-self on the back and start thinking about yourself for a change, they're b-a-a-ck!" adds Art, a genial, balding, florid-faced man. "But, hey, what are you going to do, he's your kid, you don't let him starve on the streets."

Sam doesn't stay in a job very long—he's worked at nine different marketing or consulting companies in the last eight years, and during some of his periods of unemployment he moved his clothes and his computer and his sound system back into his old room. "He can get a job, he just can't hold on to it, " Art says. "Or won't," adds his wife.

There's some confusion about why Sam keeps hopping from job to job. "Maybe he comes on too strong, maybe he's hard to work with, maybe it's a personality thing, but he doesn't usually last past the probationary period, six months or so; either he quits or they fire him. We never quite get the straight story, and we don't want to embarrass him by asking," Art says.

"It's certainly not because he can't do the work," Sherry adds. "He's very smart—he finished third in his class in college. We're not talking about low-level jobs, either; these are good jobs that start out with big salaries. The first one he had paid more that I make after twenty years of teaching. Of course, anything pays more than teaching, but still . . ." Her voice trails off.

Art, an electrical engineer, marvels at how fast this generation changes jobs. Art's worked for two employers in 35 years; the longest his son has held a job is barely a year. "The first couple of times he didn't tell us until he'd already changed jobs. After that he came home until he found another one, and that lasted a few months and he came back again. Before he got this job, which sounds like it's a lot lower on the totem pole than he's used to, he'd be downstairs, drawing up business plans, setting up meetings, trying to find people to back these ideas he had. He calls his room downstairs World Headquarters, and I say, 'Headquarters of what?' and he says, 'Headquarters of Me.' To tell you the truth, I think his dreams are bigger than he is. He lives in this fantasy land where he's going to own his own company and make a million dollars before he's 30."

"And I tell him, 'You better hurry, kid, it's gaining on you,'" Sherry puts in. Sam's working in Dallas now, but his mother isn't optimistic. "I could tell when he called me last week there's some trouble going on with this one, too. He said, 'Don't sell the house yet, Mom,' and I said, 'Honey, we missed the market, the last time we could've sold it at a profit you were living downstairs so we couldn't.'"

Sam's parents were counting on the profit from the sale of the home they bought two decades ago so Art could take early retirement and Sherry could stop teaching and they could move to Mexico and open a B&B. They have been planning the move almost since Sam finished college, going to weekend seminars on the hospitality industry, learning the fundamentals of the business—"B&B's for Dummies," they laugh, but it's clear that it's more than a fantasy. What's stopping them from realizing their dream is the prolonged process of launching their son into his own life.

Says Sherry, "I was looking through some old pictures last week and there was one of me nursing Judy when she was just a couple of months old. I remember having one of those crazy thoughts you get when you're a new mother and it's 2 A.M. and you're in that sort of maternal reverie . . . they're just sucking away and you're kind of daydreaming. And suddenly I had this image of an old woman. She was totally transparent, all dried up, with nothing inside her, and I thought, That'll be me some day, there won't be anything left of me! What a thought for a mother to have, right? Me and Medea! That was almost 30 years ago, but here I am feeling that way again. I want us to be on our own now. I want my life!"

Sparing the Help vs. Spoiling the Child

Art doesn't think Sam can make it without their continued help and support, but Sherry's not so sure. "If we didn't have a home for him to come home to, and he couldn't pay rent because he didn't have a job, would he get one and keep it, or would he end up, I don't know, working at some minimum-wage job and living in a trailer? This is something we ask ourselves a lot— actually, we fight about it on a regular basis. We've almost broken up over it; once I moved out and told

Art, 'If you're so worried about him, stay here with him by yourself.'"

For Sherry, their differences are clear: "I think we harm our kids as well as short-change ourselves by giving them so much help, and he thinks we hurt them by not doing as much as we can, even if we have to make sacrifices to do it. It seems like all the parents we know whose kids are in that sort of limbo state that Sam's in have the same question: When does helping them destroy their motivation to help themselves? Frankly, I'm tired of being all understanding and supportive, nurturing him, taking care of him. It's just not something I personally enjoy anymore. I think we'd be doing him a favor if we let him struggle instead of thinking he can give up and come home when things don't turn out the way he wants them to. Maybe he'd work harder or have more realistic goals if he didn't have us."

"But then he'd end up stuck in a job he hated," says her husband. "How could we let that happen?"

"We're the ones who are stuck, not him," says Sherry.

They're both right and they're both wrong, but their differing views reflect the two perspectives most often expressed by parents of young adults whose lives, especially as they approach 30, still haven't come together: that we "owe" it to our grown kids to continue to support them and their dreams (even if they sound unrealistic to us), or that by withdrawing our resources—financial, emotional, residential—we encourage them to be autonomous and independent. Social psychologist Terri Apter calls the former the myth of the spoiled child and the latter the myth of maturity.[6] In other words, some of us do too much for our grown kids, and some don't do enough.

Lives Without Guideposts

The life course we followed like a yellow brick road to adulthood has been destructuring in the last 25 years. Education, work, marriage, and parenthood are decreasingly connected to each other at all socioeconomic levels. Our kids' adulthood doesn't look much like ours did; it's more individualistic, less tangible, and harder to define, since it lacks many of the markers ours had—careers, mates, kids, mortgages—and the ones it has seem out of sync or not applicable to their lives.[7] Social, economic, and technological changes that have occurred since we were their age have made it harder for our kids to become the type of adults characteristic of earlier generations, even ours; each successive postwar cohort has extended its adolescence, emerging from a vague and prolonged youth into a vague and prolonged adulthood that is more of a psychological phenomenon than one based on role changes and traditional meaning. Our initial run-ins with the real world seemed exhilarating; theirs are often depressing, especially for those who've been burdened rather than blessed by the belief in their specialness that we encouraged.

While adulthood has lost much of its structure and meaning for our kids, middle age has been changing for us, too. (We call where we are now middle age, even if not many of us will live to be 120.) We are not going gentle into that good night; we're retiring younger, starting new careers, building different life structures with whatever resources and resilience we possess. Our kids aren't the only ones who feel entitled; so do we, and what's more, we've earned it. We expect more opportunities for self-development. We expect more autonomy. We, too, have an array of options for a midcourse correction or a new challenge; there's a lot we still want to do, and we're planning to stay as young as we can (for people our age, of course) for as long as we can; as one of our cultural icons sang, "Hope I die before I get old."

Leaving No Forwarding Address

Bob and Marysue put off their dream of sailing around the world on their own boat until their last child left for college. They'd no sooner put down a deposit on a 46-footer than their eldest daughter returned home, her one-year-old son in tow. "Her marriage had ended, and she was not only emotionally shattered—she was financially destitute," says her mother. "But she was in no shape to look for a job for months." During that time and for almost two years thereafter, Bob and Marysue provided not only housing but child care, living expenses, and a health-insurance policy that would cover their daughter and the baby. They also paid for Karen's therapy and job training. "By the time she and Teddy were out the door, into their own apartment, he was old enough for day care and she had a good position as a court reporter," Bob says. "By then we'd fixed the boat up so we could live comfortably aboard it, and we were ready to put the house on the market. Then Jason came home—his high-tech start-up had failed, and he hadn't saved any money when he was making it. Once he got out—about eight months after he came home—our middle kid came knocking on the door. She'd broken up with her boyfriend, quit her job, and come home to think about her future, as she put it."

They didn't feel they could turn her away. "After all, we'd let her brother and sister move back," says Marysue. "But when she kept turning down jobs because they didn't quite suit her, Bob just lost it. After she'd been back for a year, he said, 'We're moving, and we're leaving no forwarding address, if that's what it takes!'" They put their house on the market and warned the 27-year-old, who was still living there, that her "days as a freeloader were numbered," as Bob puts it. But the housing market in Seattle was in a slump, and it took almost a year before their four-bedroom ranch house sold—"For fifty thousand less than we'd planned on when we budgeted for retirement," says Marysue regretfully.

They moved onto their boat, but the world cruise they'd planned on didn't turn out exactly as they'd hoped. Three months into it, Marysue had a heart attack; fortunately, they were tied up in a Hawaii marina, not at sea, so they were able to get proper medical care. "We put the boat up for sale a couple of weeks later," Bob says. "We were just a little too old by then—even if the heart attack hadn't happened when it did, we might have cut the cruise short anyway. It's a lot more physical labor than we thought it would be. Also, I think by the time we cast off, we were too set in our ways to make such a radical change in our lifestyle. Five or six years earlier, it would have been a different story. But we didn't get that chance."

On their return to the mainland, the couple went house hunting. "We didn't want anything big enough for the kids to come home to," Bob admits frankly. Eventually they settled on a two-bedroom apartment in a water-front condominium. There's room for a grandchild to stay over once in a while, but not for a refilled nest, which is just the way the couple wants it. "Do we resent our kids for making us put our lives on hold?" Marysue asks. "Maybe a little. I guess we never thought we'd be in the parenting business as long as we were. But when it's your child, you put yourself second—that's what it's all about, isn't it?"

A generation reared on a steady supply of guilt and obligation by parents who reminded us over and over again how much they'd sacrificed for us tries mightily not to repeat that mantra to its children. "But we're also not as willing to make those sacrifices—not when they're grown up and able to take care of themselves," says Gila, who thinks a college education is all she owes her adult kids. "Should I give up what I want so they can have what they want?" she asks. "Under almost no circumstances is the answer to that. Of course, a crisis is different—then all bets are off. Then you do what you need to do—say, your adult kid is seriously ill. Otherwise, they can under-write their own dreams; it's like, I did my job, now you do yours, and write if you get work."

Not surprisingly, fathers tolerate the refilled nest with greater enthusiasm than most mothers do, a reflection of the early years when women assumed most of the chores and responsibilities of parenting, whether we worked a double shift—one at the office, one at home—or not: "Now that they're old enough to be good company, he's glad to have them home," says Penny. "He says things like, 'Why should he pay rent somewhere when we have a perfectly good spare room he can live in?' Well, he's not the one who's waiting up for him or doing his laundry or cooking him special meals. If it were up to me, he'd be living somewhere else—anywhere else!"

Regardless of how we feel about our boomerang kids, if their return to the nest without a goal, a plan, or an estimated time of departure we can live with limits our opportunities to enjoy our own freedom and preserve our autonomy, we may just have to grit our teeth and push them out.

Chapter Five

The Challenge of Independence

SOMEWHERE THERE ARE PARENTS who can't stay out of their grown kids' lives, but we're not those people. We have agendas we've waited for years to get back to, plans for the rest of our lives, or even next week that don't include them: "Don't worry about us, we'll be fine," we hasten to assure them, and as long as they are, we really mean it. We're more than content with regular phone calls and letters or e-mails (especially with pictures), visits that are long enough for catching up on their lives but short enough to get through on our best behavior; as Jane says, surveying the mess her kids and their kids have made of her well-ordered house, "I'm so glad to see them and I can't wait till they leave!"

Physical distance alone doesn't mean our grown kids have successfully separated from us. Debra left home at 20, but a day doesn't go by without a crisis or decision that requires her mother's attention; whether it's what to cook for dinner or wear to a business meeting, how to deal with a broken heel or a broken engagement, it's Emily she calls first, her advice and approval Debra needs. Patrick, age 27, still hasn't grown out of a teenager's need to needle his father; despite Don's intentions, he can't seem to spend more than a few minutes with his son before Patrick intentionally provokes him. Amy, who's 30, has been all over the world by herself, but if her parents leave town (or even their house) without telling her first, she gets nervous. And all three of Becky and Al's boys eloped, afraid that their folks might not approve of the women they married.

We may be ready to move beyond parenting, but if our adult kids can't manage their personal and practical affairs without our help, if they haven't been able to form their own beliefs, values, and attitudes but are just living ours, if they still feel angry and resentful toward us or guilty and anxious when they behave in ways they know we don't condone, they haven't left home, they're just living at a distance. And even if we want to let go, they can't seem to let us. Clinging to us in some ways and ignoring us in others, blaming us for being too distant or too involved, insisting that we rescue them from their failures (while frequently making us feel guilty for ours), our not-quite-adult kids can drain our dwindling reserves of energy and manipulate us into no-win situations. And as long as we are unable to detach ourselves from their demands, they will make us carry the past as an excuse for their troubled present.

However tight or loose the ties that bind, we want to be included by our grown kids, not in charge of them. But sometimes that's not an option. Certain forms of excessive dependence demand our attention and even our intervention; we wouldn't just stand by and watch as an anorexic daughter starved to death or a schizophrenic son wandered the streets, we wouldn't turn a blind eye to the bruises on her face from an abusive partner or ignore his suicide attempt. But even in such extreme situations, the best we can do may not be enough: No matter how much or how often we try to help them, ultimately their lives are their own to save or squander.

Strangled by Our Purse Strings

We may not begrudge the sacrifices we've made for them—and most of us don't—but once they're adults, we're no longer obliged to support them. How long we continue to underwrite their dreams and ambition is up to us—or is it? No one in my book club even mentioned Edith Wharton after we all read the story in the morning paper about the 30-year-old who won a lawsuit against his father for cutting off his monthly allowance, despite the fact that the son, a qualified lawyer with money and property of his own, had turned down several job offers, claiming they were not to his liking. The Italian court's ruling that the young man was not responsible for keeping himself "where labor conditions do not satisfy his specific qualifications, his attitudes and his real interests, so long as there is a reasonable possibility of satisfying his aspirations within a limited time, and support is compatible with the economic possibilities of the family"[1] sent shivers down our collective spine; Judy, for one, immediately canceled her reservations for Tuscany.

Unlike the Italian constitution, our legal system sets a time limit on parental obligations. Despite the value we place on our adult children's independence, we don't want it to diminish their long-term goals; if going it alone means they may not go as far, we're usually willing, if able, to help support their goals until they've accomplished them. How long that lasts depends on our resources, their resourcefulness, and, yes, our approval of their goals; while we may not share what seems to be this generation's belief in the value of extended dependency as a lifestyle, we're willing to put up with it for a while if we think it will ultimately get them where they want to go, as long as we agree with their destination.

"Why Should They Wait Till We're Dead?"

When Tim's son Chris finished college, he did what many of his friends did: took six months off and went to Europe, a graduation gift from his divorced parents, who are both writers. Then he went to work for IBM, a job he quit after a year and a half. He's 34 now, and he hasn't had what Tim considers a "real" job since.

"He's tried a lot of different things," says his father, who mostly raised Tim on his own. "He saw all his friends from college who got in on the high-tech boom making fortunes, and he wanted to, too." Chris had a steady supply of ideas about how to accomplish his goal—an Internet-based delivery service for videos and munchies, a company that matched house sitters with people who needed them, another that fixed used PCs and resold them. With some backing from Tim, his mother, and his grandparents, he tried and failed at all of them. Tim says, "I kept saying, 'Just get a regular job,' but he said, 'Look, Dad, you're a creative person, Mom's a creative person— this is how I need to express my creativity.'" Between failures, Chris bounced back and forth between his father's house and his friends' spare rooms until Tim helped him find an apartment he could afford on the series of low-paying jobs he's been able to find since the economy tanked. Tim continues to subsidize Chris's health and car insurance, his therapy, and "about half of his other expenses."

While Chris's fantasy about getting rich "no longer drives him," as Tim says, neither does the confidence and optimism with which he once approached life. That, more than anything else, disturbs Tim, which is why he made psychotherapy for his son a condition of his continued support. "I asked his therapist—with his permission, mind you—what should I do here? What would be best for Chris? Should I continue to support him, should I refuse to do anything else, should I make him at least try to pay back some of the loans I made him when he started those businesses? But the man wouldn't tell me a thing. He said, 'You will do what you will do.' I guess he's helping Chris—after all, that's what I'm paying him $150 an hour for—but he sure didn't do much for me."

Tim isn't sure whether it's Chris's therapy or just the passage of time that's helping him cope with his depression and regain his self-esteem and confidence, which have been badly battered by his series of failures—not just at business but at relationships, as well. "I'm beginning to see some progress," Tim says optimistically. "He just started a new job. It's not what he wants, but it's not McDonald's, either. I wish he paid more attention to his health and that he didn't hang around with his high school buddies anymore—most of them are slackers. But even though he still needs my help, he's getting better at managing his own life."

Tim has been fortunate enough to be able to provide it. "I grew up in a culture where that's what parents did— they helped their kids, which is all I'm trying to do for mine. They paid for college, they gave us the down payment on our first homes, and they put money into our business ventures if they had it, that kind of thing. Maybe it's narcissistic of me, but I don't want my son living on the streets, just eking out a subsistence kind of life. I have plenty for my needs—why should he wait until I'm dead to enjoy it?"

Tim is very involved in his son's life—he advises him on his health, nutrition, the kind of friends he should have, the amount of sleep he should get. "There are teachable moments, as they call them, no matter how old your kids are," he says.

Perhaps. But the one thing you can't teach or give a grown child is self-sufficiency. There are some parents who rarely let their grown kids manage their lives or pick up a check even if they can. It's a hard habit to get out of, but we must if we expect them to develop a different one—the habit of paying their own way. And there are even more who continue to bail their kids out by the checkbook, trapped in a role they'd like to stop playing but won't or don't, having confused the appropriate desire of parents to protect their young from harm with the inappropriate wish to prevent them as adults from suffering any of life's hardships. "I never expected that at this point in his life—at 34—I'd still be supporting him," Tim says. "I'm very disappointed, which he knows. But as long as he needs my help, and as long as I can give it, I will. I'll tell you, though: If I'd known being a parent was going to last this long, I might not have done it."

Codependent on Dr. Spock

On the brick-and-board shelves in the family room of Dave and Marilyn's 100-year-old converted barn on the outskirts of Louisville are the books that kept Dr. Spock company on the shelves of a generation that raised its kids in the last third of the century: *Parent Effectiveness Training; Liberated Parents, Liberated Children; Your Child's Behavior Chemistry; Your Child's Self-Esteem; Raising the Type-A Child; The Vulnerable Child; The Hurried Child.*

Despite the conventional wisdom that permissive child raising began in the 1950s, this couple doesn't remember it that way. Their childhoods were strict, their lives carefully regulated, and the pressure they felt to realize the dreams of their first-generation American parents was something they didn't want to impose on their own children. "I think we were a lot looser with our kids than our parents were with us," says Marilyn. "Where I probably differed most from my mother was believing that forcing your kids to do something by using your power or authority was wrong, that it denied them a chance to learn self-discipline. I thought that if I could just figure out what my kids' problems were I could solve them and that the most important thing I could give them was self-esteem."

She and Dave have given their children much more than that. Thom, their 29-year-old son, is one of those perpetual graduate students who can't quite settle on a dissertation topic and doesn't have to while his folks are still footing the bill for his education. Jeff, who's two years younger, was never the scholar his brother is, but he was a go-getter with big dreams, certain that despite the abysmally low salary he was earning at a high-tech start-up, his stock options would eventually be worth a fortune. Unfortunately, when the start-up shut down, Jeff ended up with no job, $21,000 in Visa bills, $15,000 more owed to his parents, a BMW he couldn't afford to drive, and an apartment he couldn't afford to rent.

Dave and Marilyn have been bailing Jeff out for a long time; he's never made any attempt to repay them, even when he might have. He hasn't worked for more than a year; he quit the last job he had, telling his parents he had "too much respect for my own spare time to ever go back into an office and burn away my days," as his father recalls. "He said it was his time he was defending—that was where his freedom was," adds Marilyn.

What Jeff's done with his freedom is hard to pin down exactly. It's easier to determine what Dave and Marilyn have, which is let him convince them that, since they're still subsidizing Thom's lifestyle, they ought to be doing the same for him. Although their more-than-comfortable circumstances have allowed them to do so without feeling the pinch, the recent downturn in the economy has them worried about their own financial security. "I look at how much money we've lost in the last two years and I go around the house turning off lights," Dave says.

He can't understand why Jeff isn't motivated to make something of himself. Like other parents who allow their grown kids to take them for a similarly long and expensive ride, Marilyn and Dave believe that how their kids turn out is a reflection of how good a job they did, not how their kids themselves performed. The money they spend on their sons, says Dave, "sometimes feels like the price we're paying for not doing something—who knows what?—when we should have." It's a telling statement, proof of their conviction that Thom's inability to finish his education and Jeff's unwillingness to pay his own way is their fault, which makes them particularly vulnerable to the emotional as well as financial extortion their sons continue to exact from them. But their willingness to assume responsibility for Thom's and Jeff's choices and failures will not help them assume it themselves. "The free ride is about over," says Dave. "It's gone on way too long already. And with the future as financially uncertain as it is, we simply can't afford it. I don't ever want us to be in a position where we have to be dependent on them— that's every parent's worst nightmare." He's told Thom that he has one more year of subsidized graduate school—"I said, 'If you don't get your doctorate by then, you'll have to pay for it yourself,' and while initially he didn't believe me, he does now. And guess what? He's gotten a job as a teaching assistant at the university— something he used to say he'd never do because it was going to take too much time away from his studies, and he's turned in the first two chapters of his dissertation."

Marilyn and Dave have told Jeff they've canceled his

debt to them. "I said, 'We'll take it out of the money we're leaving you, if there's anything left,'" said Dave. "I don't think he really believed me until I showed him the codicil I'd added to my will. And I showed it to Thom, too, and said, 'You back me up here if you have to; half that money is yours!'" They've also told Jeff they will no longer provide any financial assistance. "He's on his own—if his time and his freedom are so valuable, he'll have to find a way to pay for them himself.

"I know he didn't believe me about that, either, until they repossessed his BMW and I didn't jump in and rescue him. He was really furious. He tried to get Marilyn to give him the money, but I told her, 'Don't you dare; he's got to learn sometime.'"

According to his parents, Jeff is rethinking how much his freedom is worth and what it's costing him. "I think he's getting tired of living such an unstructured life," says Marilyn. "He sees all his friends moving ahead in theirs. He seems to have adjusted his dreams to reality—at least, he's been interviewing for real jobs lately, not just clerking in a record store for spending money." Adds Dave, "He asked me last week if I was really going to kick him out of the house, and I said, 'You've got the same amount of time your brother has—one more year.' This time, I think he believes me."

Parents Who Give Too Much

Parents who give too much do so out of their own needs, not their children's. They give out of unmet desires for love, attention, or self-esteem; they give to compensate for early deprivation (in either generation); they give to change their adult children's behavior or fill up the emptiness inside them. Because nothing their kids do can ever be enough to make their parents feel complete, as the beneficiaries of such parental largesse they will always feel inadequate. And meanwhile, they may develop a passive expectancy that other people will provide for them as well as the belief that when they do, they will have to meet a multitude of the giver's needs.[2]

Susan, a self-starter who put herself through college, encouraged her kids to strike out on their own as soon as they were grown. Divorced when her kids were teenagers, she had dreams of joining the Peace Corps once her parenting days were over. At 55, she's still not sure that day will ever come, although she first applied to the program over 15 years ago when Terry, her youngest child, was filling out college applications.

Terry's decision to go to college 3,000 miles away surprised her mother. "She always had this fear of abandonment," says Susan. "I don't know where it came from, but when she was a little girl, I couldn't even go down a different aisle in the grocery store without precipitating a crisis. But I was thrilled when I sent in the deposit on her dorm room in Boston; I thought it was her way of saying, That's over now. And maybe it was. The trouble was, saying it didn't make it true."

Six weeks after Terry left San Francisco for college, Susan gave in to her daughter's pleas, delivered daily, to come home. "Every time she called, which was sometimes three times a day, she was crying," says Susan, a slender, soft-voiced woman with wide-set hazel eyes and expressive hands that punctuate her words. "It just broke my heart. She kept saying, 'I'm miserable, I have to come home, I can't stand it.' I was frightened that she'd do something to herself. What else could I say?"

When Terry came back west, she moved into her old room and transferred to a nearby college. When she graduated, Susan sold the house, hoping it might force her daughter to strike out on her own. Terry moved into her first apartment, but it was less than a mile from Susan's new condo. "Even though she was 22 by then, she still clung to me like glue. Whenever I went out of town, she needed to know exactly where I was going to be and how she could reach me, which she did—every day I was gone. And when she went to Europe herself— a trip she'd planned and looked forward to—it was almost a repeat of her freshman year. She called me or her father every day; she missed us so much she couldn't stay away, and she flew home after less than a week."

Terry, who is a middle-school administrator, has been self-supporting for more than a decade, but she remains dependent on her mother for emotional validation, support, and approval. "I kept waiting for her to go through that teenage rebellion stage—I was longing for it!—but she never did," Susan says. "She has several friends her own age, and she's had a couple of boyfriends, but despite years of therapy—individually and together—we still haven't figured out why she can't let go of me, and I've given up trying."

A year ago Terry, whose romantic relationships haven't led to marriage or the child she desperately wanted, decided to become a single mother—after making sure that Susan agreed. "She could manage it by herself financially—she inherited money from her grandfather," Susan says. "Emotionally? I wasn't sure. Maybe a baby might help her fully wean herself from me. It was a big chance to take with someone else's life. I knew when the subject first came up that there was a possibility that if she went ahead and did it, I might have to step in and take over the baby's care if she wasn't up to the challenge. But it was a chance I was willing to take, because I knew that if Terry never had a baby, she'd be unhappy for the rest of her life, and I just couldn't bear that."

As it turned out, the baby Terry decided to have without a husband but with her parents' emotional support may have helped her become, if not totally independent, much more so than she was. For the first time in 36 years, Susan doesn't feel "on call" for her daughter. "I finally have the freedom I've been waiting so long for," she said, "but the Peace Corps isn't looking as appealing now that I have this darling grandchild a few blocks away!" While Terry still phones and sees her mother regularly, she doesn't seem to need her in quite the same way she once did.

"Would she have gone ahead and had the baby if I'd said no, you're nuts, I'm not behind you on this? I don't know . . . maybe that was a kind of test I should have made her take. But I didn't." Instead, Susan participated in Terry's decision in every possible way: She even carried the donor sperm from the bank to the doctor's office the day her daughter ovulated, and she was the labor coach when Terry delivered her nine-and-a-half-pound son.

"This baby has brought our whole family together," Susan says. "Her brothers are delighted to be the male presence in the baby's life . . . one of them moved back here after living in L.A., just so he could be closer to them. She's mended her fences with her father, whom she blamed for our divorce. And for the first time, she's making her own decisions about her life. Who knew?"

Who indeed? Having a baby on one's own doesn't seem like the straightest line to independence, but at least Terry has a back-up support system that many single parents lack. And while her dependence, like Chris's, has lasted well into her thirties, there are many others in her generation who never seem to be able to cut the ties that bind. Their inability to manage their own lives may take other forms, like anorexia and addiction, or the transfer of their dependency needs from their parents to cults or gurus. But psychological, emotional, and financial dependence all requires agreement, spoken or unspoken, between the one who is dependent and the other who is depended on.

Parents who are so enmeshed with their children that they feel their pain as if it were their own may encourage their dependence without even realizing it. Generally these parents have a lower sense of autonomy and relatedness to others; they often feel deserted when grown kids don't seek their advice or ask for their approval and see their independence as desertion. Where dependency has been encouraged, separation is extremely difficult; where the relationship is a symbiotic one, it may be impossible.[3] Parents who are adept at promoting their kids' independence share certain characteristics: They're able to satisfy their own needs as well as their children's, and they have a clear sense of their own values, especially the value of autonomy, for themselves as well as their kids.

It's questionable whether the difficulties some of our adultolescents are having with the responsibilities and commitments appropriate to their age and life stage would magically solve themselves if we weren't around to help, but if we don't take the chance of finding out, especially with the kids we've labeled (at least to ourselves) the "vulnerable" ones, we'll never know, and neither will they. Whether their difficulties in letting go are due to fear of failure, aversion to responsibility, an excessive need for our approval and attention, or just plain laziness, we need to acknowledge our role in their dependency for our good as well as theirs. If we're providing so much support and protection for our grown kids that something much more appealing than self-sufficiency is necessary for them to be willing to try life without it, we're only colluding with them in their denial of the reality of adult independence and making it even more difficult for them to achieve it. We're not used to valuing our needs and feelings as much as we value theirs—as parents, we're accustomed to putting them first and ourselves second. But until that changes, there's no real reason for our kids to give up their dependence on us, which will last as long as we let it or until it doesn't work for them any more—whichever comes first. While we cannot rescue our adult children from crises of their own making, we can and must rescue ourselves from the habit of trying to do so, or they will never be able to manage without us.

Chapter Six

⁓

Maybe We Shouldn't Have Inhaled

ONE OF THE HARDEST THINGS for any parent to accept is that no matter how much vigilance we exercise, we cannot always control what happens to our children. For even though we put plugs in all the sockets, they got shocked. And even though we put gates on top of the stairs, they fell. And even though we taught them to say no to the things that were bad for them, sometimes they said yes.

We were not the first generation to use or abuse drugs, but we may well have been the first to describe them as "recreational." Everyone laughed when then-candidate Bill Clinton insisted that although he'd tried marijuana, he hadn't inhaled—we knew better, even those of us who never did, either. Some of us told our kids the truth about our youthful experimentation and others didn't, even if they asked; better to be a hypocrite, we decided, than a bad example. Even the boomers who stayed too long at the party or never threw the bong out with the bathwater at all tried to keep their children away from drugs, although many took a "do as I say, not as I do" approach to legal substances like alcohol and cigarettes.

The gloss of nostalgia tints the recollection of our own adolescent experiences, which seemed only daring then, not dangerous, a rite of passage rather than the road to ruin. "We drank, we smoked, we got high— everyone did," said a lot of the parents I talked to (at least, the honest ones). "But nothing bad happened to us—well, not most of us, anyway—so we weren't as worried as we probably should have been when our kids did the same thing."

The Perils of Nostalgia

Almost every illegal drug available on any given street corner in America today has been around for a long time, but most of them pack a lot more wallop than they did then, particularly marijuana. There are new forms of old drugs that are more potent, more addictive, and more available than they once were; those who traffic in them are as cognizant of the changing needs and tastes of their customers as Target, General Motors, or Procter & Gamble.

The popularity of certain drugs seems to ebb and flow in response to the prevailing zeitgeist: marijuana and hallucinogenics like LSD and magic mushrooms in the psychedelic 1960s and the mellow, me-centered 1970s gave way to an epidemic of coke and crack in the fast-paced 1980s. The use of heroin and other opiates increased in every socioeconomic bracket in the let-down that followed those go-go years and maintained their hold on the drug-using population (which is mostly concentrated in that same desirable 18- to 34-year-old demographic so sought after by advertisers) even as a methamphetamine epidemic ushered in the jittery start of the millennium. "It [drug use] tends to go in cycles—uppers are followed by downers which are followed by uppers again," the director of a methadone clinic told me. "Many of the designer drugs and the 'niche' drugs we see today have been around before, under a different name."

Ecstasy, or MDMA, was called Adam 20 years ago. "I knew marriage counselors in Marin County who used it in couples' therapy to help spouses lower their barriers against intimacy, and gay men who took it at discos and tea dances on Fire Island for the same reason, " says Wendy, who's connected in both of those milieus. "The pills I took in college to stay awake and cram for exams, and those my obstetrician prescribed to control my weight when I was pregnant 33 years ago were amphetamines—the same drug my stepson went to prison for using when he was 23," says Genevieve, who admits to having had "a small problem" with diet drugs during her first marriage. *"Plus ça change, plus c'est la même chose."*

She's right—the more things change, the more they stay the same. "Whatever my parents warned me against, I had to try. My kids are the same way," said a bearded, fiftyish man I sat next to on a cross-country flight. "Except I knew when to stop and they didn't. Why is that?" It's a question that plagues many of us, one to which we have no satisfactory answer.

It's Not the Age of Aquarius Any Longer

This isn't the way Bob and Evelyn had planned to spend this evening, in the cramped basement meeting room of a Lutheran church 30 miles from their comfortable Seattle home—"so we won't see anyone we know," she admits in a whisper. It's their first Nar-Anon meeting, and what surprises them even more than being there themselves is how many other couples who might be their friends (but thank God they're not) are there, too. People like them, whose grown kids are trapped in the netherworld of drugs, strangers who've gathered to listen, talk, and cry together over their own powerlessness in the face of their children's crippling addictions and blighted lives.

It's that impotence—the inability to control what's happened to their son, to "fix" what's wrong with him— that's almost harder for his parents to bear than anything else that's happened since Larry got hooked on drugs a couple of years ago. Along with all the other emotions that are front and center in the room tonight, the frustration that can-do people like them feel is as palpable as their concern for their son.

Up to now, they haven't run into too many problems they couldn't solve or fix. Bob, a solid-looking six-footer who was a football star in college, built a small family hardware business into a successful chain of stores in three states; Evelyn, who still looks remarkably like the Tri Delt she was when she was Homecoming Queen the year Bob led his team to a Big Ten championship, turned a talent for entertaining into a small but thriving catering company. "But we never missed a school play or a soccer game," Bob says. "Probably none of them did, either," his wife comments, gesturing to the other parents who, like them, are trying to figure out what, if anything, they can do to help their kids get clean and stay that way.

It's not as if drugs are news to either Bob or Evelyn—after all, they came of age in what they remember fondly as the halcyon days of $10 lids and the occasional hit of windowpane. But they put that behind them before they had children, which helped them take things in stride when their teenagers smoked pot in high school. "We told them the truth about our own experience—we thought they'd learn something from it, " says Bob. "Of course, the dope we smoked was pretty mild. Heroin . . . God, who worried about their kids using heroin?"

Heroin is a word that strikes particular terror in people like Bob and Evelyn, because it was always a drug that "other people—not our kind of people" used. But heroin, particularly in its smokable form, has made insidious inroads among middle-class young people, all of whose parents blanch when this evening's speaker says, "There are only two places junkies end up—dead or in jail." Because a "junkie" is exactly what their 25-year-old son Larry is. And after a six-month stint in the King County jail for buying drugs from an undercover policeman, he's an ex-felon, too.

"He'll always have that on his permanent record," his mother says sadly. "Remember that? The permanent record? The one they said followed you everywhere and got you into a good college? Larry's was great until now."

Larry's room in his family's comfortable split-level home, with its view of Puget Sound and the Olympic Mountains, looks just as it probably did when he was a teenager. The bookshelves hold an impressive array of tennis and soccer trophies; Evelyn mounted and framed Larry's Eagle Scout merit badges, his National Honor Society certificate, and all his diplomas from kindergarten to college. The plaid spreads that cover the twin beds are a little faded now, and the snapshots and newspaper clippings and acceptance letters thumbtacked to the corkboard over the desk are yellowed and curled at the edges, but hopes and dreams a decade old seem to hang in the air like dust motes, a sad and striking contrast to the reality of Larry's life today.

"My poor baby," his mother murmurs as she closes the door of her son's room.

"Some baby," says Bob, more harshly. And then, "How could he do this to us?"

Is It a Symptom or a Disease?

Hoping to find an answer to that question, Bob and Evelyn have spent a great deal of money that was earmarked for their own retirement on lawyers, therapists, and an expensive rehab program that Larry walked away from after ten days. They've replayed every moment of his childhood and adolescence, wondering where they went wrong, and they've almost come to blows—or at least separate bedrooms—over their disagreement about whether Larry suffers from an awful disease (her view) or a failure of self-discipline and willpower (his). They've armed themselves with information, much of it conflicting, about how best to help their son do what they cannot, for the first time in his life, do for him.

Like many of their peers whose adult children are addicts, they've poured all their resources—emotional as well as financial—into Larry's problems, shorting themselves, their marriage, and their security as a result. They're suffering from phantom blame—the certainty that they caused the problem, even if they don't know how. They feel helpless in the face of needless waste, and betrayed—yes, betrayed—by their son's self-destructiveness. "When I think of the care I took of him, all the things I did to make sure he was happy and healthy and had everything a child needed, good food and fresh air and the trips to the pediatrician and the orthodontist, and the lessons and the tutoring and . . . and . . ." begins Evelyn.

"And then he shoves something up his nose, he sticks a needle in his arm, he takes this strong, healthy body and this great life he could have, and throws it in the shitter—excuse me," Bob finishes. "It makes you want to shake him and yell at him and holler, 'How could you do this to yourself? How could you do this to *us*?'"

Both of his parents are bewildered by how deeply Larry has hurt them and uncertain about why he has. They can't stop thinking of their son's drug problem as something he did to them rather than something he did to himself, but painful as it is, their hurt is just a by-product of his addiction, not the purpose. They want to know why he does what he does and what he means by it, but he may not know, either, and until he does he may not be able to stop it.

Family Day at Rehab

Cindy and Mark are driving through the Connecticut River valley on a verdant spring day, much like the last time they drove this route, three years ago, en route to their daughter's graduation from an Ivy League college. This time they are headed for another similarly exclusive, expensive institution, where 24-year-old Kate, who's been in residence for 28 days, will be graduating again. But not before Cindy and Mark have joined the parents, spouses, or other significant people in the lives of their daughter and her fellow graduates and met with the professionals to whom they've entrusted the care of their loved ones.

It's a meeting Cindy, for one, is dreading. She expects to be criticized, shamed, and humiliated, confronted with her inadequacies, told she is codependent, enabling, and toxic. And, like her husband, she is already marshaling her defenses, especially denial. Because while they have faced the fact that Kate drinks too much, they don't really believe she has a disease, but if she has one, it's the symptom rather than the cause of an underlying emotional disorder, and once she gets to the bottom of it, she'll be cured.

Unhappily, they're wrong; substance abuse is the disorder, not the other way around. It follows a predictable and progressive course, it's permanent and chronic, and, left untreated, it will inevitably and invariably be fatal. In fact, they won't be blamed or shamed, which might be easier than facing the hardest truths of all: that addiction is a family problem even if only one member of the family is an addict; that everyone in the family is involved, and that recovery is as necessary for them as it is for their daughter.

For the parents of an addicted young adult, recovery entails breaking through their own wall of defenses and letting in reality, identifying their roles in their kid's chemical dependence, and realizing the dangers inherent in blaming it on themselves or their child. It means understanding that no one in the family—the addict or the parent—is the focus of the problem; alcohol (or drugs) is. This approach to addiction, the 12-step model favored by many rehab centers and support groups for addicts and their families, teaches that everyone is responsible for his or her own behavior, feelings, and recovery, but what Cindy and Mark will find it hardest to accept is the fact that Kate's addiction is not their fault and her recovery is not their responsibility.

Like many other parents in the same situation, they've made valiant efforts to protect themselves from what they don't want to believe is true—that their daughter is an alcoholic. Also like other parents of addicts, they've developed their own restricted and emotionally crippling ways of coping—denial, shame, blame, and withdrawal—which are straining their marriage, disrupting their other family relationships, and robbing them of taking pleasure in any aspect of their lives: "How could we?" Cindy asks plaintively. "It's never not on our minds. We're never not thinking about how we can fix it . . . how we can fix her."

That may be our own addiction: the refusal to believe, despite all the evidence to the contrary, that we cannot fix them, that they have to fix themselves, that the only problems we can fix are those that belong to us. "I spend the first hour of every family session telling parents that, but I think it takes a long time to get through to them—sometimes years," says an addiction counselor.

Many of our grown kids refuse to admit that drugs or alcohol have run away with their lives. Others distance themselves from us because they feel guilty for letting us down and don't want us to know how out of control they are. They shrug off our efforts to help, denying they need it, insisting they're fine, repeating that they're capable of taking care of themselves even when they're clearly not.

After a particularly strained, tense Thanksgiving dinner, which ended with Kate passed out in her seat, her sister, older by two years, came clean to Cindy and Mark. "She said that everything that had gone wrong in Kate's life—losing her fellowship, breaking her engagement, being evicted by her roommate and even that car accident she said was the other driver's fault—was because she couldn't control her drinking. It was the first we knew how badly off she was—of course, she didn't live at home, so how could we?" says Cindy. "At first I didn't believe it—Marcia's always been jealous of Kate. But then I began to put things together in my head—the way she slurred her words sometimes when I'd call her, all the times she tripped over her own feet and sprained her arm or her ankle, the car accident. It wasn't like I hadn't been paying attention. My mother had MS, and it showed up in some of those same ways in the early stages. I never told Mark how worried I was that maybe Kate was getting it, too; I guess some part of me didn't want to face that possibility unless I had to. So I blew off Marcia at Thanksgiving. Then Christmas came, and Kate was so drunk she couldn't see straight. The next day we brought up her drinking, begged her to get help, offered to pay for it, did all that. When she got really abusive with us, we knew Marcia was right."

Unable and unwilling to stand by and watch their daughter destroy herself, they got help from a professional and staged an intervention. Cindy, Mark, and Marcia, plus Kate's former fiancé, her best friend, and her graduate adviser confronted her, describing the times, events, and behavior that led to their concern. They told her how her drinking was affecting their lives—especially Mick, who still loved her and wanted to marry her, according to Cindy—and offered her a choice between the two treatment programs they'd settled on after Marcia did an Internet search, consulted several experts, and visited both residential clinics with her parents.

Kate refused to consider either one. She denied that she had any problems she couldn't solve herself; she could stop drinking, she told them, and she would. They countered with the questions the intervention specialist had suggested—the "what-ifs," as Cindy enumerates them. "What if you do start drinking again? What if you have just one more? What if you can't control yourself?" Kate had a ready answer for every one: "Don't worry, I'm fine." Says Mark, "That intervention was a total failure."

In fact, while it may not have gotten Kate into treatment, it wasn't the failure Mark believes it was; it showed Kate she wasn't alone and that help and support were available to her, although it was several months before she accepted it. "We had to let her come to it herself," says her mother. "Even if we'd been able to force her into treatment, which of course we couldn't, it wouldn't have done any good."

When our kids are still under our care and control, we may be able to force treatment on them. But once they're grown and gone, so is our power to do anything except make help available if and when they ask. And even if they never do, we must seek it ourselves, not for their sake but for our own.

Coming to terms with addiction in the family proceeds from denial and disbelief to accepting reality: understanding that we are powerless over our children and their addictions and that while their lives may be unmanageable, ours aren't. Learning to understand and accept the situation means removing ourselves from the position (or the belief that we're in the position) of being in control, and learning to tolerate our inability to change the course of their lives.

Staying Out of Their Program

Even when it's their problem, their disease, many times we have a hard time allowing them to solve it in their own way, which is often by trial and error. "You can only work your steps, not theirs," says Shelly, the mother of a son who recognized that he had a drug problem long before he told her. Ben had been living on the opposite side of the continent since he was 20; seeing her son only once or twice a year, for short periods of time, Shelly had no idea that he'd been struggling with an addiction to cocaine for four years.

During that time he'd tried everything to cure his habit: AA, NA, Rational Recovery, methadone, even a rapid detox program involving a protocol he'd read about on the Internet. But he couldn't seem to get traction; he kept backsliding, again and again.

He dreaded telling his mother about his addiction—Shelly, who raised him alone, had made him the center of her world for years, and even though he'd moved 3,000 miles away, he still was. Finally, though, he couldn't keep it a secret; when his dealer threatened to kill him if he didn't come up with the money Ben owed him, Ben sold the last of his possessions, skipped town, and flew home.

Learning about Ben's addiction was an enormous shock, but Shelly, a self-made woman used to tackling problems head on, immediately swung into gear, finding an inpatient drug treatment clinic and borrowing the money to pay for it from her retirement fund. When Ben completed the three-month program, he moved back into his mother's house while he tried to restart his career and his life.

Meanwhile, Shelly kept a close watch on his progress. She kept tabs on how many meetings Ben attended, called his sponsor when she suspected he was using again, voiced her concern and suspicions about his friends, left books and pamphlets and newspaper clippings about addiction on his bed, checked his pockets and his bureau drawers for indications that he was back on cocaine, and generally treated him like a child instead of the adult he was. Well-meaning as it was, her overinvolvement with Ben's recovery came close to sabotaging it.

Many parents feel as though their grown kids' recovery is their business, too. "You can't just stand by and watch their life go down the tubes," says Cindy. But offering help—even paying for it—doesn't give us the right to interfere. If we can't stay out of their program, there's a good chance they won't stay with it.

Doing the Wrong Thing

When denying that our grown kids are chemically dependent no longer works, our first impulse is to help. Galvanized into action by what we now recognize is a threat to their happiness, if not their lives, we take over, as Shelly did, rendering them powerless over themselves as well as their addiction and undercutting whatever efforts they've made, or are making, to help or heal themselves. Taking over control of their out-of-control lives takes away the responsibility to solve their problems that rightfully belongs to them and puts it, instead, on us. While we do so out of the best of intentions, for their own good, we're really just continuing to "enable" their dependency. Shocked, stunned, and scared, we revert to treating them like children, which simply infantilizes them and transfers their dependency from a drug to us—at least temporarily. But the best thing we can do for them—if we have the courage—is nothing . . . at least, not right away.

That's a difficult task if we've made a habit of rushing in and rescuing our kids, no matter how old they may be. But in this case—as in many crises—nothing is the right thing to do. Few of us know enough about addiction to understand it, and few of us know our children well enough to understand theirs. Although we once may have had a pretty good idea of their strengths and weaknesses, it's out of date now, because we don't know the lessons their life beyond our reach has—or hasn't—taught them. When we look at our grown children, what we see is usually a sentimentalized picture of the youngsters they were, not the adults they've (almost) become. We don't know when, why, or how they got into this hole or what kind of help will enable them to pull themselves out of it.

Often the first actions we take are the wrong ones—blaming, criticizing, and giving advice before they've asked for it. Until we've made ourselves as knowledgeable as possible about chemical dependency and learned to rein in our impulse to take over the control they so clearly have not been able to exercise themselves, whatever we do is likely to be counterproductive. And even if we manage not to blame or criticize them, we probably won't be able to refrain from blaming or criticizing ourselves.

While focusing on us instead of on them is a wise alternative to doing the wrong thing, even for the right reason, blaming ourselves is not. Educating ourselves about their problem is different from trying to solve it. And for education we must go to the experts, who can tell us what we need to know, particularly about how nature and nurture—genetics and the environment—

combine to make some people particularly susceptible to what really is a disease, not simply a lack of self-discipline. Finding a support group to help us cope with our feelings is just as important as arming ourselves with information; being with other parents who have been and are still going through what we are, who can let down their defenses and confront their denial, encourages us to follow their example. Groups like Al-Anon and Nar-Anon can help us understand our role in our children's addiction and in our separate but equal recovery.

While psychological counseling or therapy of a more conventional kind can be useful to chemically dependent people, it often focuses on addiction as a symptom rather than a cause of the problem. Eventually all addicts will have to get to the underlying issues involved in their dependency, but doing so before they stop using whatever substance has them in its grip may just be a way to avoid doing that and provide them with more excuses to continue.

Therapy for us, however, is another matter. It may be the first step we take in admitting to others that our child is an addict, which is the only way to get the support we need to cope with the feelings of shame and embarrassment inherent in such an admission. A psychologist's office may feel like a safe place to mourn our losses; a therapist can counteract or at least mitigate our tendency to assume guilt, blame, and responsibility for our children's problems and help us understand the family system that contributed to them.

Because we're dealing with ourselves, not our kids, it may seem like "doing nothing" to educate ourselves about addiction, understand our role in it, and find support in the company and wisdom of other parents like us. But in many cases, it may not only be the right thing to do—it may be all we *can* do. Regardless of what happens to them, we have to take care of ourselves, so that when and if they're ready to receive our help, we're able to offer the right kind.

Chapter Seven

The Limits of Love

IT IS A TRUTH (almost) universally acknowledged that our grown kids have the right not only to live their own lives, but also to screw them up. Since that isn't a right we granted them, it's not one we can take away; as Simone de Beauvoir tells us, we must recognize their liberty, even in failure. But that isn't much comfort when we watch them make choices we know—we absolutely, positively, no-doubt-about-it know—are the wrong, foolish, or dangerous ones. Even the sense of vindication in "I told you so" (whether we just think it or even say it) doesn't alleviate our concern, calm our fears, or ease our disappointments: what good is being right if our kids are scared, stuck, sick, sorry, or unhappy?

Some of the ills that befell them were beyond their control as well as ours, although knowing that is not the same as believing or accepting it. Understanding that addiction is a disease rather than a failure of willpower may make sense intellectually, but it's an emotional gut-check when we know that if they hadn't foolishly put themselves at risk they wouldn't have caught it in the first place. Realizing that depression is a mental illness, not an excuse, and that our kids would really rather be getting on with their lives than sleeping them away or walking through them like zombies is hard to keep in mind when we're certain that if they just got out of bed or put a smile on their faces and gave it the old college try, they'd feel better. And accepting that for reasons that neither we nor they may ever know or understand, they grew up vulnerable enough to be seduced by a charismatic cult leader or victimized by a sadistic partner or compelled by an obsession or controlled by a psychosis requires more faith, wisdom, perspective, forgiveness, and serenity than most of us possess. The only thing that makes sense is that it doesn't make any sense, and in spite of all our intellectualizing, we may never be able to comprehend it.

Paying a Different Kind of Attention

Just like our kids, we have the right to live our own lives and make our own choices—including how we respond to the reality of theirs. We can choose to deny or accept them, support or reject them, condone or condemn them. We can involve ourselves or stay on the sidelines. And we can lie—to ourselves and others—or tell the truth.

Those, of course, are the extremes of what most of us actually do when we're forced to recognize that our kids are not who we wanted, hoped, or expected them to be. What we ought to be doing instead is paying attention to who they really are.

Sometimes we will be shocked into recognition, the way Gretchen was when she saw her anorexic daughter after a year's absence or Larry's parents were when he was arrested for attempting to buy drugs. Other times our feelings will nudge us toward taking a closer look at behavior we may not have been acknowledging or have even made Herculean efforts to ignore or suppress, as Suzanne did with Josh's expensive watch. Evelyn shudders at the word "junkie" and quickly substitutes "recovering addict," which sounds a lot nicer. But it's really just a way of deluding herself into believing her son can take drugs or leave them. Barbara will tell you that Tommy's mood swings are just his personality, that he's creative and sensitive and passionate and high energy. All that may be true, but the last time he was this manic he called the FBI to tell them he'd figured out who the men on the grassy knoll were. Sylvia doesn't really believe her daughter got that black eye by walking into a door, any more than she believed that she tripped over her shoelaces and fractured her arm, but probably Lizzy provoked it, and surely Tom would never intentionally harm her or the children. Amelia thought Gia was just a picky eater until she weighed 92 pounds and had to be fed intravenously. But naming is knowing, and knowing is necessary to decide what we can or should do next.

Denying the Undeniable

Retreating into denial is an understandable defense against believing something we desperately don't want to believe about our kids. And that brings up a subject that someone wiser than I am, or at least more sensitive or politically correct, might not raise here, at least not right after a few paragraphs on addiction, mental illness, domestic abuse, or anorexia. (Have I left out criminal behavior?) Homosexuality has nothing in common with any of those conditions or situations. (Have I made myself clear?) But that doesn't mean it's something most parents jump for joy about it. When Roberta married out of her race and faith, her parents tried to dissuade her. "There are enough problems in marriage, why do you have to go looking for more?" they asked. She hadn't thought about that for years, but when her son told her he was gay, it was the first thing that popped into her head; fortunately, she managed not to say it out loud.

Those nudges from our feelings or hints from our intuition may eventually motivate us to come right out and ask our grown kids what we may have been wondering for a long time. "Part of me wanted to let her know it was safe to tell me, that I was all right with it," says Kay. "The other part wanted to hear her say, 'Oh, Mother, don't be ridiculous, of course I'm not gay.' But I knew. I always knew."

At least when Hannah came out of the closet, Kay didn't attempt to push her back in: Julie met 23-year-old William's declaration that he was gay by telling him of course he wasn't, and Ethel and Max told Steve, 27, it was just a stage he was going through; Ethel still gives his phone number to any single, attractive, unsuspecting young woman she meets. Erin told Peter he might be bisexual, but he certainly couldn't be gay—everyone in their family was straight. Virginia and Cal refer to Anne's partner as her roommate and tell each other and anyone who asks that Anne, who's 34, just hasn't found the right man yet.

Sexual orientation is not something our children choose—it chooses them. They (and we) have no more control over or responsibility for it than anything else with which they came into the world—the color of their eyes, the shape of their ears, perfect pitch, or an interest in taking small household appliances apart and putting them back together. I know that, and you know that, and so do all the experts, except maybe the fundamentalist fringe that think it's an "alternative lifestyle," or worse. (Alternative to what? Jean wants to know, on her way to Florida to lobby the legislature on gay rights, specifically on her gay son's right to be a foster parent. It's certainly an alternative to living in a closet and hiding who you are, she declares.)

The Real Truth About Gay Pride

Homosexuality Is Like Greatness, says the bumper sticker on Jean's Volvo. You Don't Choose It, It's Thrust Upon You. But deep in the hearts of a number of even the most educated, sophisticated, liberal baby boomers we remain to this day is a sneaking suspicion that maybe that's not necessarily so. For reasons we may or may not think we know, some of us suspect or are even convinced that our kids—especially our daughters—have chosen their sexual "situation," a word Lexy prefers to "orientation" or "identity." "You don't have to be Jerry Falwell to think, maybe with the right kind of help, at the right time, or even the right guy, things would have been different," she says wistfully and defensively.

Even if there were the teensiest possibility that was true, it still wouldn't matter. As a matter of fact, social science generally agrees that human sexuality exists along a continuum of gay to straight and that most people place themselves on that continuum depending on the sex of the Other who arouses their erotic interest, something people also have no control over. But so what? No matter what experts we listen to, no matter how well adjusted we or they are to the reality and/or permanence of their homosexual or lesbian identity, our hearts will still ache, because we know it will likely make their lives harder in many ways and because we will feel cheated out of our dreams—not just for them but for ourselves.

There are parents who fight, as Jean does, for their gay kids' legal and social and civil rights to be who they are, which is a worthwhile and important endeavor. Some stand beside and behind their own gay kids and open their arms and hearts to others whose parents have turned away from them. A few cling to the hope that this is just a stage their adult children are going through, so why bother telling the relatives? And many, many more accept their kids' sexuality without trying to fathom it, let alone attempt to dissuade them from it—parents who cherish their gay kids and welcome their partners and lovers into their lives and their families. There are also parents whose kids' homosexuality never bothered, worried, or disappointed them, says Julie, who wishes every gay son and daughter, especially hers, was lucky enough to have one. But, as she's learned, and would be the first one to tell you, in the end it doesn't matter how you feel, what matters is what you do; she's been acting As If (it's perfectly normal, it never upset her, et cetera) for so long that she hardly ever bursts into tears in front of the Baby Gap window the way she once did, realizing she'll never buy onesies for a grandchild.

Following the Pied Piper

Making my way slowly through airport security a few years ago, I paid little attention to the orange-robed young man with the shaved head, tapping a tambourine while his pretty if blank-eyed companion thrust leaflets into the hands of my fellow frequent flyers. Then I took a second look. I know that girl, I realized; I used to pick her up at six in the morning with her skis and sack lunch when she and my daughter, third graders both, were in Mogul Mice together. I searched my mind for her name, but I could only remember Barbara, her mother, who opted out of the car pool because she was afraid to drive on snowy roads but knit matching mittens and hats for the kids of the mothers who weren't. It was Barbara I felt for, not her daughter—Barbara and others like her, whose kids transfer their dependence from us to cults, gurus, or self-appointed messiahs, and remain as adults in totalist milieus that promise enlightenment or eternal life in return for the surrender of self, the renunciation of ties to their families, and wholehearted allegiance to a life and lifestyle that frightens and confuses their wounded, worried parents.

Simon was a Stanford junior when he followed a sweet, pretty, soft-spoken girl he met in a Palo Alto coffee shop back to a house in the nearby hills for dinner with her family, which turned out to be a group of her fellow Moonies. The next time Jack and Mary heard from Simon, he was calling from a Moonie house in Tulsa; the time after that he was in Washington and, less than a week later, in Georgia. "They kept him on the move, always one step or a few states away from the last place he called from," Mary said, "and his phone calls were always monitored." They hired a deprogrammer they heard about from their priest to wrest their son back from the Moonies' clutches, but the former cult member was arrested while attempting to return Simon to his parents; the right to free association is guaranteed by law, Jack said bitterly, "even when there's nothing free about it." Simon still calls home from time to time, but Jack refuses to talk to him. He is bitter that his son has "thrown away his life," and is angry at his wife for her continued and wholehearted involvement in a support group for families of cult members. He dismisses it as "the blind leading the dumb," disappointed that Simon "would rather beg on the streets" than come into the business Jack spent 25 years building. "He's not my son any longer," he says, "just some brainwashed zombie."

Charlotte's 33-year-old daughter, Shay, lives in a "spiritual community" in Arizona with the two children she's had by its leader—two of the nine he's fathered by other women in the group, according to Charlotte, who says, "I will never understand it. Of all the places I ever thought my daughter would end up, this wouldn't have even been on my radar screen."

Charlotte, a chic, frosted, polished-looking woman in her fifties, has had ample opportunity to interact with the man her daughter calls "my master" since she moved to Phoenix to be closer to Shay and her grandsons five years ago, after she and her husband divorced. She's made a new life here, representing area jewelers whose work she sells to galleries and boutiques all over the country from her sun-filled patio apartment. A fax machine clicks away in her office, which is where Shay sleeps occasionally when she spends the night, as she did for a week after Charlotte's recent heart bypass surgery. In another room are twin beds that Charlotte bought for Shay's sons, who are no longer permitted to be alone with their grandmother since she tried—and failed—to get custody of them. "It took a long time for Shay to forgive me for that," Charlotte says. "Almost as long as it's taken me to forgive her."

Shay, who was a popular girl who did well in school, graduated from a prestigious college, and attended graduate school for two years, does not fit the image most people have of the typical cult member: a lonely, confused, vulnerable, naïve young adult. She was 24 when she first encountered the man who would change her life. "The first we knew of it was when she told us she was dropping out of her Ph.D. program and going on some kind of retreat in the desert to decide what she was going to do with her life," her mother remembers. "Two weeks later she said she'd met a wonderful man and was staying in Arizona with him."

That was the last time Charlotte and her husband heard from their daughter for almost a year, when she called to tell them she was going to have a baby. "Of course, we were stunned! We had all kinds of questions, ranging from who's the father to when can we meet him and when are you getting married, or are you? She said, 'Well, I'm not,' and we took a big gulp and said, 'Fine, dear,' because really, what can you do? She said she'd write and tell us all the details, but she didn't, and finally I said to Nick, 'We're going out there and see for ourselves.'"

They flew into Phoenix, rented a car, "and then realized we didn't have any idea where she was—all we had was a post office box number in a little town about 30 miles away," remembers Charlotte. "So we went there, and when we told the postmaster we were looking for our daughter and told him the box number, he looked at us strangely and said, 'Stick around, if you think it'll do any good—somebody usually comes and picks up the mail for that box at the end of the day, you can follow 'em back there.' We asked him what he meant, but he just shook his head and said, 'I can't tell you anything else.'"

Years later, Charlotte shakes her head, recalling her naïveté when they followed a husky young man in a pickup truck to their reunion with Shay and their first meeting with their grandson. "Looking around, my first thought was, Well, this isn't so bad. A few buildings, all freshly painted, a big garden, and a couple of tractors, and lots of people around—probably 50 or 60, plus some children and babies. It looked like your basic sixties hippie commune, only cleaner. That's what we thought at first. Shay wasn't exactly surprised to see us—she knew once there was a baby involved, we'd show up there. She had him in her arms, and once I saw him, I forgot everything else. But then she said she had to go to a prayer service, she'd see us after or we could come if we wanted to, so of course we did, although I wasn't letting that little baby out of my sight! As soon as this man got up and started talking, I knew—I mean, he may be a manipulative, egotistical, insane man, but he was extremely charismatic. And it was obvious they all thought he was God. What he was saying made no sense at all, it was this quasi-religious bullshit, plus a lot of paranoia about the government, but Shay was totally mesmerized. Nick turned around and said to me, I think we've lost her, and he was right—we had. It just took me five years to realize it."

Unable to convince Shay to come back to their hotel with them that evening, to abandon her "master" even temporarily, Nick and Charlotte returned to Phoenix and mobilized themselves. "We talked to two lawyers, the police, the local FBI office—which referred us to the Cult Awareness Network—and we even called our senators and our congressman. But they all told us there was nothing we could do—she was an adult."

In the next three years, Charlotte and Nick divorced and Shay had a second child, another boy. Both Charlotte and Nick made several trips back to Arizona, individually and together. "Our marriage had been on the rocks for a long time before that—I think we held on until we finally grasped that we had no power over things, that Shay was beyond our control, and by then we'd just run out of steam," Charlotte says. Convinced there was nothing she could do to "save" her daughter, Charlotte bent her efforts toward rescuing her grandsons. "I'd wake up at night thinking about Waco and Jonestown and Heaven's Gate," she says. "I used to call Nick, even after we broke up, and just cry. I mean, we have our own lives now, but she's still our daughter, they're still our grandchildren." Although the specter of Waco "still haunts my dreams," she adds, "I have stopped trying to get Shay to leave him or the community. The more I try to, the more she pulls away from me. And I have already lost enough to that son of a bitch."

She comforts herself with the knowledge that her daughter seems happy, and her grandsons are healthy, inquisitive, well-mannered children who return her love. "There are people out there whose families have turned their back on them, but I could never do that. I used to believe that some day Shay would wake up and see what a charlatan he is and how she's wasted her life, but I no longer think that will happen. The boys, though . . . that's another story. I'm here for Shay, but I'm really here for them."

An Alternative to What?

Not every so-called alternative community is a cult, whose most basic feature is the control of human conduct within a controlled environment. Any ideology may be carried by its adherents in a totalist direction, according to Dr. Robert J. Lifton; his psychological criteria against which a cult environment may be judged include milieu control, extensive personal manipulation, the division of the world into the pure (the group) and the impure (everything and everyone outside it), coerced confession or other acts of symbolic surrender, the maintenance of an aura of sacredness surrounding the basic doctrine or ideology, language loaded with thought-terminating clichés or all-encompassing jargon, the assumption that doctrine or ideology is more true and valid than any aspect of human experience, and the dispensing of existence—those who are not in the group are bound up in evil, are not saved, and do not have the right to exist.[1]

By those criteria, relatively few organizations classified as cults are really cults or dangerous to their members' physical or emotional well-being. Many spiritual, therapeutic, or other "intentional" communities (like the communes that flourished in our youth) that practice or promote specific values or behavior, ranging from homeopathy to organic farming to conscious child-raising, represent a paradigm or point of view about how one should live in the world that seems alien, and thus frightening, to us. "I just want her to live a normal life," says Bonita, whose 25-year-old daughter, Lara, has been in an ashram in India for the last four years, ignoring the fact that the life her daughter is leading is not only "normal" but highly respected in cultures where leaving home and pursuing a spiritual life as a nun or a monk in early adulthood is a widespread practice. To Bonita, Lara's freely made choice feels like a betrayal of an unconscious and unspoken agreement about how she would proceed with her life; to Lara, her mother's position may seem like a betrayal of a different unspoken agreement: "I thought you loved me unconditionally, irrespective of my choices."[2]

Stepping outside of our own cultural biases and trying to view our kids' lifestyle from a wider perspective requires that we move past our social stereotypes and try to see our adult kids for who they are, not who we hoped they would be. One of our most prevalent stereotypical beliefs is that everyone who lives an alternative lifestyle is being brainwashed or unduly influenced by their group or its leaders. But we are all subject to the influences of the particular culture to which we belong, to our religious leaders or political philosophies. In some cases the only difference is that one set of ideologies or leaders is agreed on by the majority of the culture, and the other is agreed on only by a minority. It's not up to us to decide which influences are beneficial to our kids and which are not, or even to understand the whole of their perspective if they choose to live according to principles and practices that are outside of (our) contemporary mainstream culture. It *is* up to us to support and respect them, or at least to act *as if* we do. Acting *as if* may seem like a lie, but the message it conveys more accurately addresses the essential truth of our relationship with our kids—that we love them, even if we don't love their choices. The agreement to disagree encompasses both our differences from our grown kids and our desire for continued connectedness on whatever shared ground we stand on together—in other words, to have relationship in the areas where relationship is possible.[3]

Who Are the Victims Here?

When our kids behave in ways we consider unethical or immoral—"when they turn out to have shitty values," as

Linda puts it—we're confronted with what it's hard to consider as anything other than our own failure to teach them right from wrong, which, next to nurturing and protecting them, is one of a parent's most important responsibilities. If Linda's son has a moral compass, she is yet to discover where true north is: He has been conning and cheating his way through life since his adolescence. Marina's daughter is unfaithful to her husband, Patrick's son is a bigot, Clemmie's eldest sells term papers to college students who pass them off as their own work, and Paula's son is a deadbeat dad whose refusal to pay court-ordered child support, which he can well afford, prevents her from seeing her grandchildren. Many of us know there are skeletons in our kids' closets and choose not to pry them open. "I know enough things about how he operates, I don't need to know more," says Linda. "He's my son and I love him, but sometimes it's very difficult. It feels like he's a kid who's sticking his tongue out at me going, 'Nyah, nyah, I'm bad and you can't make me be good.' Well, I can't, and I've just had to accept the fact that even though I showed him the right path, he took the wrong one."

Judith's son seems to have no visible means of support, yet he drives a nice car, lives in a luxurious apartment, and buys her extravagant gifts at Christmas and on her birthday. "I know he's selling pot—at least, I hope that's all it is," she says. "I've never asked him directly; I just hope he doesn't get caught." Cate's daughter, a statuesque blonde, goes on a lot of trips with wealthy, older men; "She'll come back with a new piece of expensive jewelry and show it to me—I don't ask what she did to get it, because I'm afraid she'd tell me."

Letting go of our grown kids means letting go to anywhere—even beyond the law or inside its prisons. Of all the ways our kids can and do mess up their lives, for many parents this is the most humiliating, shameful, and inexplicable road they might have taken.

Parents whose kids have run afoul of the law feel judged. "If you saw my son led away in handcuffs, probably the first thing that came to your mind wouldn't be I bet his parents brought him up well," says Nan, whose fast-talking, charmingly convincing Matthew defrauded dozens of people out of their life savings in an elaborate scam for which he was sentenced to 15 years in prison.

They feel resentful. "They both did the crime, but only my kid did the time," says Stuart, whose son went to jail for stealing industrial secrets while his erstwhile partner, who sold them, turned state's evidence and got off with a slap on the wrist.

They even, sometimes, feel like the real victims of what they consider "victimless crime," which, reflecting the values and experience of our generation, usually means anything that has to do with sex (although not of the violent, coercive, or exploitative variety) and, especially, drugs; it's how Marcy talks about her daughter's arrest for buying and using cocaine, but it's also the phrase David uses when discussing his son's arrest for selling it; a gram at a time, he adds, not by the kilo, and never to children, which is what he told the judge at Dave Jr.'s sentencing hearing.

We may come to their aid with lawyers and/or psychiatrists, or bring any influence we might have to bear on the disposition of their illegal doings. We may remain convinced of their innocence, despite evidence to the contrary. We probably will offer excuses or explanation for their actions: They might have done whatever it was that led them down this path, but it wasn't on purpose; it was a symptom or result of psychological trauma or vulnerability; it was because they were or are mentally ill or impaired by drugs or alcohol, or even convinced by the coercion or influence of others. Regardless, once the courts and the jury have rendered their decision, our kids—who are adults in the eyes of the law, if not in our own—are out of our hands, beyond whatever control we once believed we could exert over their behavior.

We may even be relieved, if not of our shame or blame or embarrassment or suffering, at least of some of our fears; as Rosie says of the son whose drug-fueled crime spree led to his imprisonment, and as Margaret says of hers, convicted of raping his girlfriend, and as others who've struggled with adult kids who are out of control have come to conclude: at least we know that they are where they can't harm themselves or others.

We have watched our dreams fall apart, betrayed by the children we raised to know better. We feel helpless in the face of needless waste, frightened when we think about what the future has in store for them, ashamed in front of our friends and neighbors. Catherine, a regular churchgoer, sneaks into early Mass and leaves before it's over so no one will see her, and Pat tells people his son, who's doing time for armed robbery, works for a secret government agency, which is why he couldn't come to his sister's wedding. Good, caring, committed parents all, unable to reconcile the ideal child we hold in our hearts with the one in the orange jumpsuit who sits across from us at a table, separated by shatterproof glass and a life we never imagined could turn out this way. Love them though we do, support them though we may, and hope as we must that they can bear the consequences of their actions if not learn from them, we are forced into realizing that we can do no more for them now than they can do for themselves.

Forgiving the Unforgivable

Confronted with the loss of our dreams, we will keep rewinding the movie of their childhood to see where it went wrong, to isolate the moment when we might have changed the course of their futures, and of course, to affix blame. We may hold on to our blame or anger because it's the only thing that still connects us to them, but, in fact, anger is a solitary position that makes us feel apart from, not closer to, our kids. Describing how her anger at her son for his criminal behavior builds up the week before her monthly visit to Matthew in prison, Nan says, "It's kind of like PMS—by the time I see him, I spend the first 10 minutes begging him to forgive me!

"If I could tell other parents who've been through this, I'd say, Stop blaming yourself for what happened to them," she adds. "It was their actions, not yours, that led them to this place; you are not responsible. Assume you did your best and stop blaming yourself for not being good enough to prevent whatever happened." In trying to understand what motivated her son to do what he did, Nan attempted to look at it through the lens of his values, rather than her own: "When I realized that he saw this whole thing as a business deal that went bad, not a crime—not like holding someone up with a gun, say—I was able to say, that's not what I taught him. By the time he was 10, he knew right from wrong. So what he did, he was responsible for it, not me."

Wherever it's affixed, blame is a barrier to forgiveness, which is both a choice and a process. Many parents become estranged from grown kids whose choices and values are simply unacceptable to them. When there is nothing to be done or said that will repair the torn connections, they may abandon the relationship. Like Jack, they remain unforgiving to punish their kids for hurting them or destroying their dreams. Whether their betrayal was in what they did or how we perceived it, feeling betrayed matters more than being betrayed, particularly when what is betrayed is the assumption that their ethics and morality are the same as our own.[4]

If our goal is to seek revenge on our kids or convince them to see things our way, or hold on to conflict, pain, and anger until they see the error of their ways, we are likely to remain estranged from them. When our hopes are tempered with a more realistic assessment of what might still be possible in our relationships with them, if not in their lives, it is easier to let go of our fear, resentment, and anger while still continuing to love them—the very essence of forgiveness.

Forgiving our kids their trespasses against our values, our hopes, our assumptions and expectations is a gift we give ourselves, not them. Forgiveness allows us to let go and move on after grieving not only the loss of our dreams for them but also those we had for ourselves. And that is a task that falls to us in this season of our life regardless of whether our grown kids are exactly who we always hoped they would be or not.

~~

Chapter Eight

Separating from Their Problems Without Separating from Them

HAVING SPENT OUR FIRST ADULTHOOD hoping our kids will make it to theirs without mishap, embarking on our second with the realization that they haven't, we are faced with the problem of what to do next, how to do it, and whom to do it for.

In their study of women who faced what they called "unexpected, untraditional and unacceptable behavior" in their adult children—including mental illness, crime, cult involvement, eating disorders, drugs, and suicide threats—sociologist Jo Brans and Margaret Taylor Smith identified six stages in the coping process: shock, attention, action, detachment, autonomy, and connection.[1]

Most of us manage the first three, some better than others: Blessed are those with troubled kids who know Carrie, or someone like her, who can not only find you the best whatever-it-is you need—counselor, shrink, doctor, lawyer, deprogrammer, group, protocol, clinic, program, or hospital—but can also be counted on not to ask why.

It's the last three stages we often get stuck on, but unless we get through them we will never arrive at that state of emotional equilibrium Judith Viorst called Permanent Parenthood, when we are able to "live with our fierce and undiminished love for our children, while making peace with the limit of what we can and can't and shouldn't try to do for them, while making peace with the limits of our control."[2]

There is little most of us wouldn't do to help our grown kids straighten out their lives, but, unfortunately, as we will learn when talking to the experts, there is also little we *can* do. Legally adult, our sons and daughters have a right to make their own decisions—even sick, stupid, deluded, wrong, and irrational ones. We may wish they'd get treatment for their problems, but as long as they're not a danger to themselves or to others, we can't force it on them—and even if they get it, it may not be effective. We may find the "experts" who might help them, but we can't drag them to their offices—and even if we could, they have to want their help. We may offer them shelter, but we can't make them come in off the streets—and even if we did, they wouldn't stay.

In the absence of any obvious explanation, it may be difficult to put our finger on exactly what is wrong with our kids, particularly those who've failed to thrive. We may have only our feelings, our gut, and our intuition to guide us in deciding whether it's our problem or theirs that's aroused our concern. If our overriding feelings are resentment, anger, and frustration rather than fear, worry, and alarm, chances are we're reacting to what we see as their immaturity, poor judgment, or failure to act responsibly, the result of which infringes on our rights, resources, and privacy. If we're mad because they can't leave home, get a life, make a commitment, stick to a goal, or settle down, we may be expecting more than they can deliver and reacting angrily to their failure to grow up according to our timetable. If we feel put upon, blamed, abused, or taken advantage of because their behavior is straining our marriage or other family relationships, threatening our financial security, and limiting our autonomy, we may be ready to be done with parenting and get on with our life.

Our resentful, frustrated feelings are a good indication that how we feel is our problem, not theirs. The best thing we can do is refocus our attention from them to ourselves, decide what practical support we will provide for them and for how long, and set appropriate limits on what we will permit or allow, something we can't do unless we are truly free of guilt or responsibility for that behavior. We may feel cheated by their inability to realize their potential, but that job is theirs and the problem is ours.

If, on the other hand, we're frightened, alarmed, or worried—if our parent radar is pinging because they seem depressed, angry, volatile, or alienated, emotionally unstable or physically vulnerable—it's likely that there's something serious and potentially dangerous going on. In that case, our only option is to try to find out what's causing their problem, offer what help we can, accept the current realities of their life, and make a conscious choice to detach from the source of our pain—not them, but their problems.

Tuning in to our feelings allows us to own them, admit them, and interpret the message they're sending. We need to trust even our negative feelings as valid sources of information rather than distort or deny them or convert them into somatic disorders like headaches, high blood pressure, and sleep disturbances. Most studies of parental well-being confirm that parents' mental health is dependent on events in their adult children's lives as well as in their own and on the nature of the parent-child relationship.[3] The content of the relationship has a significant effect not only on parents' psychological health but also on their sense of burden; negative or problematic relationships can cause feelings of meaninglessness, agitation, and psychiatric symptoms in parents. Those whose grown kids are mentally ill or addicted report high levels of depression as well as stress and worry, sometimes experiencing overwhelming waves of hopelessness and despair, concern for their child's future, or anger at their disruptive behavior. Not surprisingly, grown kids' problems, especially their psychological ones, are a more important predictor of depression for women than most other variables; they create more anxiety, depression, and emotional drain for mothers than fathers.[4]

Our feelings often contain elements of both fear and anger, especially when our grown kids' lifestyles, values, and interest in being in relationship with us are very different from ours. Even while recognizing their right to live and behave as they choose, it's possible to feel worried, disappointed, betrayed, and abandoned; what's really impossible is *not* feeling any of those emotions. But if we can set our own values aside and keep our issues out of their process, accept what *is* rather than demand what *could be,* avoid the minefield of what can't be resolved and build instead on what we still have in common, it will be easier to own our own pain and disappointment instead of burdening them with it. The only way we can keep them close—in our hearts if not in our homes or daily lives—is by putting as much distance as we can from whatever is the cause or symptom of their difficulties. Our most important task, as parents and as people with lives of our own, is to separate from their problems without separating from them. And the only way we can do that is by managing the difficult task of detachment.

The Key to Our Survival

Detach, literally, means to let go of. Detaching is the only way we will survive the pain, frustration, and disappointment of our lost dreams for our children.

It is the first step in reclaiming our lives.

It is the acknowledgment of the limits of our parental responsibility and the acceptance of the fact that we have done as much as is humanly possible for them.

It is the realization that whatever we forgot to do for them—to teach, show, notice, praise, give, or honor—they must do for themselves, or do without.

It is the only possible hope for their independence.

It is the only route to ours.

We may not be able to detach in every area of their lives—some may continue to need our financial or even physical help, especially if they're ill or impaired. But even while providing it, we must strive for emotional detachment, which, in the words of Brans and Smith, "frees our child from our definition of his life, and . . . turns his life over to him to do with as he will."[5]

Detachment demands that we rethink our priorities and shift them from our kids to ourselves. It requires us to see them for who they are, which is not us, even if she has her mother's gift for languages or he is the spitting image of his father; we are separate individuals with separate lives on which neither has a permanent claim. Our detachment forces them to take charge of their own lives. It allows us to go on, despite the fact that our questions about why this happened to our kids—and, yes, to us—will probably never be answered. Detachment teaches us about tolerating the intolerable, the inexplicable, the paradoxical—not just in our kids, but in the world. Detachment allows us to take pleasure in the moment, even if those we love are in pain. Detachment allows us to support our kids with our love, which is all we have left to give them, and stay connected to them even if we don't agree with or understand their choices. Detachment makes it possible to focus on the love we feel for them while putting aside our efforts to persuade, manipulate, or control them; to recognize when circumstances are out of our hands and "let go and let God," as the old hymn has it. Detachment is our only hope for living a different relationship with our kids instead of clinging in vain to an old one.

Detachment isn't a by-product of too many years of pain and disappointment, although that's how it may seem; it's a conscious choice, the expression of our own will to survive. And while it may seem like a lonely stance, what it really is is the decision to put an end to our suffering and lay down the burden of our disappointment.

Melanie is a poster girl for detachment. Her daughter, Cat, an addict at 16, got clean long enough to produce a beautiful son, whose custody was granted to Melanie eight months later when Cat was arrested for buying cocaine from an undercover cop. After a jail term and her third treatment program, Cat embarked on a career Melanie describes, without a trace of embarrassment or irony, as a "sex worker."

Now 33, Cat has been drug-free for three years; when she became pregnant again, Melanie helped her find and pay for a new apartment for her growing brood. Cat has given up stripping and enrolled in community college; occasionally she goes off for a weekend with a well-to-do "friend," usually timing it with Melanie's once-a-month weekends with her grandchildren. "I don't ask where she's going or with whom, not even once when she came back with a full-length leather coat," says Melanie. "I've got her cell phone if I need to reach her. I don't ask if she's going to classes or even to NA meetings. I don't ask if she's seeing anyone. I don't ask if there's anything she needs. I'm like a lawyer—I don't ask questions I don't know the answers to."

Melanie has worked two jobs to pay for lawyers, therapists, rehab programs, pediatricians, and rent deposits. "I've lost a lot because of Cat's problems—money, jobs, and relationships as well as peace of mind. I've had a man I loved walk out, finally, because he couldn't deal with it when Cat called me from jail to bail her out or showed up loaded for Thanksgiving dinner and nodded out on my couch. But every time my girl's really tried to make it, I've been there for her, and I always will be."

Melanie has set limits on what she will and won't offer or put up with. "I said, 'You can't use drugs at my house, and I want my key back.' I don't loan her money, although of course I still buy clothes and toys for the kids—I am their grandma, after all, and I love my weekends with them; I'm glad if she's getting a little relief, but that's not why I do it, I do it for me. I don't know why a girl with her brains and looks and potential and, yes, really good mothering turned out the way she has, and while I pray she turns her life around, that she really has this time, it's out of my hands. I wish I could count on her, but I know I can't. I don't know if I'll ever be able to, which is pretty sad."

She doesn't wonder much anymore about the reasons why her daughter made the choices she did. "What could I do about it now?" she asks rhetorically. "Sometimes I think about her sad life and get so torn up I have to yank my thoughts away from going in that direction, like you'd yank a horse's reins. I'll be running, usually, and I just force myself to repeat the mantra—I am not her, She is not me. I try to remind myself that we are not the same person—she's flesh of my flesh, she came out of my body, but she's not me . . . she's *not* me. Her life is very different from mine. I have a good job, nice friends, a satisfying relationship, my own home, my good health—all the things she doesn't have, although she's working on them. I'm not apologizing for what I have or what I've accomplished—I worked hard for them, and I'd give them all up in a New York minute if it would make her okay. But it won't. She's the only one who can do that. Meanwhile, I help her out as much as I can. I don't judge her, I just love her. And I try to do what my minister suggested—let go of my disappointment, dream my own dreams for myself, and let hope be a surprise."

Thank You for Sharing

There are two one-size-fits-all options for us that can be useful and effective regardless of the nature of our kids' problems. One is to get help for ourselves, and the other is to define the limits of our involvement with our troubled adult children. (Notice the sentence structure here: with our troubled children, not our children's troubles.)

Even if we've exhausted all sources of help for our kids, chances are we haven't begun to explore those that offer help for us. By now we may have forgotten that the best teacher is someone else's experience, but once upon a time we got the most useful, field-tested advice about dealing with our kids—not to mention support, empathy, and understanding—from other parents. That is still a valid option, if we can only get over our shame and embarrassment. When Nina suspected that her son was addicted to drugs, she boldly phoned a woman she'd never met but heard about from a mutual friend: "I think my son has a drug problem, and I understand you've had some experience with this with your own. Would you be willing to talk to me about it?" When Dan's daughter was diagnosed with bipolar disease, he mentioned it to his racquetball partner and was stunned to find out he had a daughter with the same condition and, what's more, knew several other parents whose kids were similarly afflicted.

While professionals can help us and point us toward other sources of support, no one but another parent, who's been where we are, and maybe still is, can fully understand our feelings. "I once made the mistake of admitting to a friend that I sometimes wished my son was dead, that it would be a relief if it was over, that I couldn't stand the pain one more day," says Betty, whose son, under the influence of methamphetamine, has committed several violent crimes. "She hasn't talked to me since." At night Betty tosses and turns, picturing herself at Dick's grave. "It would be terrible. I would mourn him forever. But he's hurt so many people . . . at least there'd be an end to that, to waiting for the other shoe to drop or the next horrible thing to happen. At least there'd be closure."

Betty's feelings, so incomprehensible to her friend, are understandable to those she's grown close to in her Nar-Anon group. "If I can't accept the darkest part of me, I can't forgive myself, let alone him. I was never a spiritual person, but I've learned that forgiveness requires a leap of faith, and it's your decision about whether or not you make it. What I've learned from the people in my group was that I have a choice to continue to suffer and let suffering destroy me, too, or make that leap."

Many parents have found strength and sustenance in structured, formalized family support networks and advocacy groups, which exist for almost every problem, disease, condition, or situation; only an Internet Google search or an 800 number away, they offer not only information but also relief from the pressure to put on a good front for other people (even, sometimes, our spouses) and the easing of our emotional burdens that comes from sharing and admitting them.

Telling friends, colleagues, employers, and other family members what's happening opens up closer sources of support. Relieved of the stress of keeping a secret, our embarrassment will disappear once we realize that no one is judging or blaming us—they just want to help. Sure, some of them might be privately thinking what it's humanly impossible not to think when we hear of someone else's misfortune: There but for the grace of God go I. But that only reminds them, as it does us, that much of life is out of our hands.

It's more common for women to reach out to others for this kind of emotional feeding than it is for men. Many, but not all, men are uncomfortable with any confidante other than their wives, who then find themselves in the position of nurturer rather than nurtured. "I end up comforting him, which is the way it's always been," says Cathy. "I wish he had someone else to turn to—it's all I can do to keep putting one foot in front of the other myself. All I want from him is acknowledgment that I'm hurting, too." Says Deb, "He puts this impassive, stoic face on whenever I cry, so I turn away from him. And I know that he's dying inside the same way I am, but of course he can't acknowledge it. I find myself getting furious with him because he won't open up."

Finding the right person to talk to—someone who nourishes us emotionally and can tolerate our anxiety rather than attempt to relieve it—isn't easy. It takes a certain level of detachment to feel someone else's pain and not be overwhelmed by it; even if a buddy isn't critical or judgmental, he or she may be scared by our feelings, like Betty's friend, and unable to stand or contain them. A good "container" calms us and makes us feel that we are okay, communicating support without dwelling on our problems, discharging our anxiety and replacing it with the feeling that things are under control even when they aren't. A good confidant is an active but not intrusive listener, someone who can let us talk without needing to play I Can Top This or dwelling on his or her own problems or misfortunes. "That's why I go to a shrink—I don't have to give her equal time," says Peggy. Though many friends may offer us advice about what to do with or for our kids, we can get that from other sources. What we need from a friend is not criticism or judgment but patience and empathy and the ability, ultimately, to make us laugh, because if we can't laugh, we might as well be dead.

But we can't wear out even our closest friends, including our spouses, by making their problem or our pain or both the sole subject of our relationship; at some point, once the immediate crisis is over, we will have to pay our dues in the friendship, too.

Like Peggy, many of us turn to therapists to hear, validate, and contain our feelings. We do it because we're a therapy generation in a therapy culture, and because we may be more comfortable paying for emotional support than asking for it from other people. As Joan says, "When you vent to your friends, the unspoken agreement is that you'll reciprocate. With a shrink, you're off that hook—it's about you, not them. If you want to spend your hour crying, that's up to you. And that's what I do—I just sit there and cry while she hands me the Kleenex."

Marriages Under Fire

Problems with grown kids drive some couples apart. "He is the kind of man who needs someone to blame, and usually I'm it," reports Claudia. "I feel like I'm being doubly abused—by my child and my husband. I hear a lot of that in my Al-Anon group. Many of the people in it have had their marriages fall apart under this kind of pressure."

Grown kids' problems challenge parents' ability to support and console one another without blaming or scapegoating. While adult children's residence in the family home may provoke marital conflict because husband and wife have differing opinions about allowing or encouraging it, it's not usually associated with parents' psychological well-being[6]—in fact, coresidence is a mixed blessing, reflecting the greater intensity of our relationships with our kids in terms of the social support we get from and give each other and in role strain, which is how satisfied we are with being parents and how often we feel bothered or upset because of our kids.

Crises test the most enduring relationships, but those involving adult children impose a particular burden because they often occur at a time when our marriages are coming under renewed scrutiny, part and parcel of the reconsolidation of identity that takes place in the second half of adulthood. "Our marriage was running out of steam before Shay got involved with that man and his followers," Charlotte says. "We were on the brink of divorce then, something we would never have considered when she was younger. That was the unwritten part of our marriage vows—that if we had kids, we'd stay together until they were grown, no matter what happened. The stuff with Shay probably delayed the divorce for a few years, until we realized there was nothing we could do to 'save' her. People think that was the reason we broke up, but it wasn't. It was just the first opportunity we had to think of what was best for us rather than for her."

Because we had a different ideology than our mothers did about what constitutes appropriate roles for women, we rarely feared the advent of the empty nest. Still, while all the recent research on this stage of life indicates that it is a period of renewed happiness and vigor in most marriages, continuing parental responsibilities—financial, physical, or emotional—can drain even the best relationship of the energy we need now. Energy to invest in new roles, explore other aspects of identity, deal with retirement or new career options. To cope with the deaths of parents and other structural change in the family And to accept—or not—the physical changes that happen to even the most vigorous and age-defying among us. "It was either pay for his third rehab or my first face-lift," says Sonia. "I decided it was time to do something for myself, since I couldn't do anything else for him."

Our experience of the empty-nest transition is influenced by how dependent we feel our kids are on us. "Even when they're out of the house, they're not really gone if they're not independent," says Jane. "If your first thought is still about what they need rather than what you need, the nest is still full."

But if we have already settled happily into life beyond parenthood and begun to take advantage of the opportunities it offers for renewal and growth as a couple as well as an individual, our disappointment will be particularly acute when it turns out that our kids weren't fully or successfully launched after all, or that their problems are serious enough to hinder or delay us in getting on with our new lives. How serious is that? It depends on how much we allow their problems to stand in the way of our other satisfactions and pleasures. We won't make our kids any better or happier by being miserable ourselves, and we won't solve their problems by being in perpetual service to them; in this life, at least, being a martyr offers few pleasures.

Blurred Boundaries, Loving Limits

Defining the limits of what we can and will do for our adult children encompasses more than knowing ourselves and just how much we can give, take, or put up with and what we expect our kids to do in return. Help that's contingent on the recipient's will or ability to abide with conditions might have worked long ago—no chores, no allowance—

and works today if one is trying to borrow money from a bank, for example. But when the transaction is between a parent and a grown kid, and the only "security" we have is their promise, however well intentioned or even grudging, to comply with our demands, those rules rarely apply. Giving an addicted child money on the condition he or she uses it to buy food or pay rent is far from a sure thing, as many parents soon realize. But even in less clear-cut scenarios, the line between helping and enabling may be just as blurred, especially when we immediately respond to their call for help of some kind without first determining whether we're the first, last, or only lifeline available to them, not to mention the right one.

Our kids may have other sources of support besides us. Instead of automatically taking charge, even in a crisis, we need to step back and see who else comes forward—their spouses, lovers, friends, siblings, or employers—and respect their role in our kids' lives and their willingness to help in whatever ways they can. By spreading the burden around, we avoid bankrupting our kids' own support system. Being informed about what other help is available—including public or private aid, grants, and programs—acts as a brake on our impulse to deplete our own reservoirs of support. One person, or even a couple, can't be a safety net all alone; there's a limit to what we can do, bear, or carry.

But What About the Grandchildren?

According to the most recent Census Bureau statistics, more than 2.9 million grandparents are currently raising 4.5 million children, and other relatives are raising an additional 1.5 million children whose parents are unable or unwilling to do so. "I wouldn't and couldn't abandon these babies to foster care," says Sharon, who traded in her compact car for a van and turned her home office—once her daughter's bedroom—into a room her 3- and 5-year-old grandsons now call their own. "While there has been a drastic retrenchment in our plans for this time in our lives, there have been some rewards, too."

She enumerates them: "Watching them grow and develop. Having the house full of laughter again. Feeling closer to my husband, who now has the time and interest to be the kind of parent he couldn't be when he was building a career and on the road so much of the time. Knowing I'm making a difference in their lives. Staying in shape instead of being a couch potato—you have to, just to chase them around. Learning all the new stuff about raising kids, not just the ideas but the stuff! Making new friends, even though we're probably 20 years older than most of the boys' playmates' parents. Working out a better relationship with my son-in-law, who's not in a position to have full-time custody but has really grown up and is making an effort to be part of their lives. And seeing the smile on their faces when they wake up in the morning."

Stepping in to assume the only responsibility for our kids' messed-up lives most of us can't turn our backs on will certainly curtail our freedom to reshape postparenthood according to our heart's desire. "But if we don't, who will?" asks Lee, whose daughter left her child with her three years ago for what was supposed to be a week-long retreat to "reconsider her options" after her husband walked out on her. Since then, it's turned into a de facto guardianship Lee at first resisted but now sees as an opportunity to rectify mistakes she herself made as a mother.

"Of course, I don't really know what mistakes they were, but there must have been some, or how could she have turned into the kind of mother who'd walk out on her child?" Lee wonders.

We don't know what, if anything, we did wrong the first time. But we shouldn't be motivated to care for our grandkids out of a misguided need to do penance for our sins—real or imagined—against their parents. If we do it, we do it out of love, need, and kinship, and because there's nobody else who can, *at least for now.*

There is always the chance—a very good chance, in fact—that at some time our kids will be ready to take over again. And that's when the letting-go is truly bittersweet, because the future is leaving us along with the present.

We can choose not to take on our children's children for any or many reasons. It's important that one of those reasons, however, not be to punish our children, because innocent victims get caught in the generational crossfire; the most innocent are the grandchildren, who've done nothing that requires penance or deserves punishment.

In the best of cases our grandkids will be raised in safe, secure, loving circumstances, with two parents who are equally committed to their well-being and able to provide it. And we'll have the chance but not the obligation to participate in their lives, the joy but not the responsibility of caring for them, the luxury but not the necessity of supporting their dreams.

But these are not the best of cases. We are not being given a second chance at parenthood; although circumstances may place us in loco parentis for a time, it's probably not going to last forever. Most of our kids want to raise their kids themselves, and although they may need our help, we need to support their desire to do so by not interfering, even and especially when there are three generations of us under one roof. Taking over our children's role as parents undermines their self-confidence and infantilizes them, making them children again in their own eyes as well as in the eyes of their kids. Even if we're only partially helping by providing residential, financial, or child-care help, we owe our kids the respect one parent grants another.

Our kids, troubled or not, have the right to make their own mistakes with their own offspring; we had our chance with them. We may be footing some of the bills, but that doesn't automatically confer the right to call the shots. We can support our emotionally or financially strapped kids by backing them up, not taking over for them, and by respecting them as parents, not treating them like children.

When our kids are in trouble, we may be the only source of stability for youngsters whose personal world is falling apart. What our grandchildren need from us most is reassurance that they won't be abandoned, that they're not the cause of their parents' problems, and that they can't solve them. What our kids need is support for their efforts to rebuild their lives.

Sometimes the life arrangements our children make limit our access to their children, especially when our child is the noncustodial parent. Judy, whose former daughter-in-law was once like, well, a daughter to her, is now barred from seeing her grandchildren, because Bob, her son, is behind in his alimony. Judy's convinced it's a ploy: "She thinks we'll cough up the dough because we adore the kids. And we do, but we won't, because that's Bob's responsibility, not ours," she says sadly.

Kendra has become a fundamentalist Christian who disapproves of her parents' unorthodox ways, so Ken and Margie, who are, respectively, gay and living with a lover, rarely get to see Kendra's twin girls.

But Roz, whose son Gordon fathered a child by a woman she never met until after Tyler was born, has not forsworn the joys of grandparenthood simply because Gordon's moved on with his life. She has made her own relationship with Tyler's mom, who allows her to be as much a part of his life as she wants to be, which is considerable, especially because they live on opposite coasts. Showing off a T-shirt illustrated with a magic wand–wielding princess and the words "The Fairy God Bubbe," Roz tells me it's a recent gift from Tyler's mother, a woman who never married into her family but remains an important part of it. Divorced herself when her kids were very young, Roz remembers what it's like to be a single mother. "Without my parents' emotional and financial support, we would have gone under."

For a long time, Roz paid Gordon's court-ordered child support for Tyler. "It killed me that he was doing to Tyler what his father did to him," she says. "Not just abandoning him financially, but ignoring him in every way. I got furious whenever I thought about it, the way I used to when his father treated his kids that way. I was unable not to bring it up with Gordon, not to analyze or second-guess him, not to nag him. It got so we couldn't even talk to each other without fighting about it. It was destroying my love for him, and it sure felt like he hated me, too."

While Roz stopped paying the child support—"That's between my son and the court," she says—she remains closely connected to Tyler and his mother. Tyler spends a few weeks every summer with her. "He comes to see me, not his dad," says Roz, who lives near her now-married son. "Sometimes Gordon sees him and sometimes he doesn't. I know how much it hurts Tyler, but that's his burden to bear, not mine. All I can do for him is love him, and that's all I can do for my son, too. Eventually they'll work out some relationship, I suppose, but I can't be in the middle of it."

Things have improved considerably since Roz stopped trying to "fix" the relationship between her son and his son, and since Gordon and his wife had a child of their own. Tyler, who sees Gordon more often these days, has gotten to know his half-brother, Zack, too.

"The jealousy he expressed when Zack was first born isn't there anymore," Roz says. "It's been replaced by real tenderness—Zack worships Tyler, and Tyler returns his affection. Tyler also seems to have accepted the fact that his father will sometimes disappoint him; after a vacation we all took together, Tyler said, 'Too bad Dad didn't grow up before he had his first kid—lucky for Zack he's finally gotten around to it.'"

Phantom Guilt and Other Crimes of the Heart

Defining the limits of what we can do or tolerate isn't the same as "tough love"; it's about our survival, not their redemption or recovery. If we continually put their needs first and ours second, the reason may be as much about us as about them. We may still be attempting to expiate that "phantom guilt"—the feeling that we failed them, though we're not sure how. If we think that sacrificing our security or happiness is an appropriate sentence for our imaginary crimes, we can't set the kind of boundaries that let us reach out a helping hand to our children without becoming part of the problem rather than part of the solution. If we fear that there's not enough to keep us together as a couple besides our kids' problems, we may not be able to let go of those problems. And if, like Bob and Marysue, we "keep the light on" for so long that it's too late to put our plans for our second adulthood into action, we will never be able to accomplish the central tasks of that life stage: reclaiming, redefining, and reinvesting in ourselves.

Chapter Nine

⁓

Reinventing Our Lives: The Challenge of Postparenthood

PARENTHOOD IS ONE LONG EXERCISE in relinquishing control, or the illusion that we ever had it. Postparenthood, by contrast, is about acceptance. Our adult children are who they are—which is not to say they may not change, for they surely will, for better or worse, but to emphasize that even if we once could, we can no longer influence their behavior, values, or character. True acceptance frees us from getting stuck in the hope that they'll turn their lives around, deal with their problems, and face the responsibilities of adulthood; while acceptance may seem like passivity, it is anything but, since it liberates us to create our second adulthood our own way, with nothing holding us back.

The developmental tasks of postparenthood require us to let go of *Why?* and concentrate instead on *What's next*—not for our kids but for us. Our responsibility now is to discover purpose and meaning in other areas of our lives. Replacing old roles with new ones isn't as easy as it seems. Though others will and do love us, no one else will ever gaze up at us with a dreamy toothless grin, as if we hung the moon, and although our recent experience may have—must have!—taught us the limits of our power and influence, for many years we were in control or, at least, in charge.

With the possible exception of the first fine careless rapture at the beginning of a love affair, no other relationship in life is as all-consuming as parenthood. That's both the good news—we may not be ready to be helped across the street yet, but we're really, really tired of being on permanent call—and the bad news—what could replace it?

To start with, there's our marriage or intimate partnership, which may be perking along just fine, thank you, but could probably use a little R&R—reevaluation and reinvigoration. Even people whose kids grew up and left the nest on time and eased into their adult life without a hitch rethink what else is keeping them together when their children aren't. If that's all there is, it may not be enough to do the job: As Charlotte says of her marriage to Nick: "Our only unfinished business was Shay, and that had really been finished—our part of it, anyway—for years."

By the time our kids are in their twenties, we may have already acted out the stereotypical midlife crisis: bought the Porsche; restyled the body; chased youth down the street, thought about marrying it, and decided—or not—to stay with the one who brought us to the party the first time. Or we may have been waiting for the kids to be safely launched into their new lives before starting ours over and feel restless in our marriage because it's run out of steam but we haven't.

Postparenthood marriage is, or ought to be, a whole new ballgame. We may be using the same equipment and playing on the same field, but we need a new set of rules that speaks to our willingness to support our partners in their search for meaning and purpose and to adjust our attitudes and expectations about what our second-stage marriages should look like, how they can meet our individual needs as well as our joint goals, and what roles our grown kids will play in them.

Reinvigorating the Postparenthood Marriage

All postparenthood marriages go through a period when issues and conflicts that may have been ignored, suppressed, or papered over in earlier years resurface. While couples usually report relief and satisfaction with the empty nest, data reveal that this may be only a temporary artifact of having surmounted the initial stages of that life transition. Yes, there are marriages that don't change in significant ways at this time—but often what that means is that the couple hasn't confronted the changes that are going on around them or the need to reconsider arrangements and ways of relating that have worked in the past but may not be wholly satisfying now.

Up to this point, we've been operating on the basis of the roles we've evolved and allocated in our marriages. Whether we move from a child-focused marriage to a sole proprietorship or a partner-focused marriage, our parental roles have been drastically reshaped and redefined by our kids' adulthood, however troubled or trouble-free. The roles that take their place will not be as easily identifiable and, furthermore, will of necessity be much more fluid and flexible. While once one of us did what the poet called the work of love and the other the work of life, that may not necessarily reflect our present individual interests and capabilities. We will always be their parents, but "mother" or "father" no longer connotes our identity or determines how we relate to each other and to the world at large. Now we are two (or one) people whose roles, and thus our relationship, are up for grabs. Liberated from the constraints

181

of parenthood, we will take another look at our mate and judge whether the love between us is strong enough to sustain us for the rest of our lives. If we stay together, it will be a conscious, active choice, and we will both be willing to make the necessary accommodations, those that free us to take back the energy we invested in our kids and invest it instead in ourselves.

Not all marriages survive the empty nest; those still dealing with the problems of grown kids face a particular set of difficulties. The decision on how and what kind of support to offer must be jointly made and carried out if we are to present them with a united front and leave them no room to manipulate us or set one against the other, something most kids, including the problem-free ones, learn how to do early and often. We need to agree not only on whether they can come back to live with us and under what conditions, but also on how much money, time, energy, and emotional support we're prepared to provide, since all of these are marital assets that under other circumstances would be available to and shared by husband and wife. Martina gives her 30-year-old, chronically indebted daughter money she doesn't tell Tom about, agreeing with him all the while that it's time Jeanne learned some fiscal responsibility. Dot keeps bad news about their grown son's recent trouble with the law to herself, because she "knows" her husband can't handle any more. Pat knows about his son's impending divorce but hasn't told Mary because he knows she'll side with her daughter-in-law—in fact, he's spent so many hours closeted away on the phone with Jim, or meeting him for a drink after work, that Mary wonders if her husband is having an affair.

New Wine in Old Bottles

Rejuvenating our careers, finding work that connects us to the world, nourishes our creativity, uses the skills we have, and requires us to master new ones will restore our vitality and answer our need to "matter," something that becomes increasingly important as we age. As a generation, we're very used to the limelight, and there's no reason to think we'll accept being unseen and unheard now. Watch out, Gray Panthers, fresh reinforcements are on their way!

Securing our future will occupy more of our attention than we once thought it would at this point in our lives, thanks to the collapse of the 1990s boom; our 401Ks are 2001Ks now, and some who took early retirement will have to come out of it, or at least adjust their expectations. "I don't mind being old, I just don't want to be old and poor," says Bev, whose pension disappeared with the rest of Enron's assets. Dusting off an old teacher's credential, she's back in school again. "I couldn't have lived on this salary when I was younger, but I can now. At first I was doing it for the money and health insurance; now I'm doing it for the kids, which is really what teaching is all about." Freed of the competitive success-striving that characterized our previous careers, not needing to earn as much as we once did, unconcerned with status-seeking and uninterested in political gamesmanship, we will bring a different kind of enthusiasm to work that is freely chosen and done with our fullest attention, a Buddhist concept that speaks to our spiritual as well as material needs.

Second adulthood requires that we reclaim those aspects of ourselves we put aside in the interests of our children and use them to re-create ourselves. "I think of it as putting new wine in an old bottle," says Ellen, who's talking about her recently acquired Ph.D., not the face-lift she had before she realized it was her insides, not her outsides, that needed updating. Bob, whose youthful idealism disappeared along with his hair, found it again building houses for Habitat for Humanity; he also discovered the pleasure of working with his hands, and now he's turned his basement into a woodworking shop.

Recognizing the limits of our parental role and seeing our children's lives as their problem to be solved, not ours, we can take charge of our own destinies, which are no longer linked to theirs. There are avenues for growth, change, and happiness that were not available to us during the parental emergency of our child-raising years, and while change will happen whether we welcome it or not, growth, like happiness and suffering, is a choice.

The personal goals we surrendered in favor of the goals of our families probably aren't the same goals we have for ourselves now; the Life List of someone over 50 isn't as long or ambitious as someone whose whole life is ahead of him. But what sociologist Jo Brans[1] calls the birth of the second self demands that we turn back to the only lives for which we are now responsible—our own— supported by our capacity to cope with change, our ability to come to terms with compromise and adjust our hopes and dreams, our faith in the healing processes of time and nature, and our ability to understand and communicate with other people.

What makes that birth possible is the resilience we have developed over years of dealing with their ups and downs, and the long view that comes from having lived over a half century or more. A post–9/11 mental health campaign that offered ways for New Yorkers to cope with stress, sadness, and depression suggested that people spend time with senior citizens because "They've seen so much in their lifetime it gives them perspective." We may not agree with that label (unless it will get us a discount at the movies or on the bus), but it reminds us how helpful it can be to reframe the problems facing our kids in the context of an entire life, not just a piece of it. Neither they nor we may ever be able to laugh about the situation they're in now, but we can't allow it to claim more than its due or define who they or we are. Although we can find neither purpose nor meaning in what has happened to our kids, we can find both in our response to it.

Now that we have paid what psychiatrist David Gutmann calls our "species dues"[2]—the psychological tax levied on us that restricted our freedom, transformed our instincts, and subjected our needs in the service of meeting theirs—there is enormous personal freedom available to us to reshape and redefine our lives. The sharp sex distinctions of early parental adulthood blur in postparenthood; we are free to reclaim those aspects of our gender that have been submerged for many years in our roles and duties as well as the pleasures and potentialities we relinquished long ago in the service of our parental responsibilities.

Postparenthood nudges us out of traditional sex roles and aids us in reclaiming those tendencies and qualities that were repressed or sublimated in our first adulthood. All the data on this stage in life suggest that the sharp distinctions of gender that prevail earlier in life soften as we age, as both men and women reacquire certain aspects of the other gender and move toward psychological androgyny. Women's maternal sensuality, passive mastery, and relation-centeredness yield to mature sexuality that is untethered from reproduction; personal autonomy and independence that is no longer linked to the needs of children, assertiveness, and active mastery, which calls on all the executive capabilities and management skills acquired over time or pressed them into service in the accomplishment of new goals. Now we can tolerate and even enjoy the aggressiveness that once might have frightened our children and alienated our husbands or partners; with renewed energy, we are less needy for and admiring of male assertiveness.

Men feel the duality of human nature in this season of their lives, too; what's been called "the emergence of contra-sexual potentials" allows them to reclaim the feminine side of their psyches: tenderness, sensuality, nurturance, and relational qualities as well as the full range of feelings. The self-love and self-idealism parents renounce, transform, and concede in the interest of the emotional needs and demands of their children becomes available in its mature form to both genders in postparenthood—a healthy, positive narcissism that energizes this new phase of self-development, which is marked by clarity and a sense of renewed purpose; a real power surge for both men and women.

The developmental view of aging does not ignore the fact that separation and loss are inevitable and that adjustments must be made to the waning of physical strength and sexual attractiveness, the capacity for procreation in women and some loss of sexual vigor in men. But as recent advances in neurobiology indicate, our brains compensate for physical aging with the ability to form new connections, new mental structures; as the old adage has it, wisdom and cunning will always triumph over youth and strength. As Dr. Gutmann writes in his wise and wide-ranging study of men and women in later life, many seeming losses of this period, much like those of earlier life, can be seen as the precondition for further advance. As the psychophysiological systems that serve the parental emergency phase out, they reveal a previous physical and psychological organization, uncovering a body/mind format that is fitted to stable social and physical environments: "Younger individuals have bodies and impulses that lead them to relish and provoke change; older people have bodies and appetites that lead them to relish and sponsor the equally vital dimensions of social stability and continuity . . . the task of experimenting and provoking social change and new social forms is generally assigned to the young, [but] the task of maintaining social continuity—the constant beat of the social heart—is generally assigned to the elders."[3] Dr. Gutmann's study, however, does not take into account the proclivity of this generation to keep right on experimenting and provoking; as we've redefined every institution that's touched our lives, we're redefining aging. We may not be marching as often or demonstrating as loudly, and the idealism that marked our youth may be tempered with reality, but we're not as interested in maintaining society as we are in reshaping it in a more equitable and humanitarian fashion.

Different Times, Different Agendas

The differing agendas of men and women in later life pose additional opportunities in postparenthood; women who have limited their career aspirations because of child raising often find new possibilities in the work they've been doing or channel their energy and ambition into creating an entirely different scenario—a change of purpose, an entrepreneurial adventure, a different pace and pattern to life. Men who have committed themselves to their work and perhaps begun to wonder, *Is that all there is?* start coming to terms with their professional accomplishments or limitations; some get out their golf clubs while others explore different options, enterprises, or careers. Both men and women become more inward-looking at this time, which doesn't mean we withdraw from other people, just that different habits of mind, like reflection and reconsideration, become a more significant part of our emotional repertoire. Knowing that we own ourselves, as psychoanalyst Robert Gould suggests, frees us from the false assumption that there is no death or evil in the world, a perception that forces us to transcend possessiveness, control, and competition: "It does not happen immediately. But the life of inner-directedness finally prevails."[4]

Shuffling the Deck for a New Deal

Since the first boomer turned 50, a gazillion books, articles, and experts have "spun" what their authors (who clearly haven't done the math!) persist in calling middle age. They've made it so appealing that the only honest response is Shakespearean: They doth protest too much! Yes, there are some great things besides senior citizen discounts that come with age—perspective, wisdom, and ego integrity, which in a fair fight would beat youth, beauty, and potential every time, but not many people would pay to see it!

We bring to what I prefer to call "later life" two conflicting urges: to take the hand we've been dealt and to shuffle the cards again. This is the choice that faces us in every aspect of our lives once our kids are grown; in fact, it always faces us, but age and circumstances demand that we make it consciously and conscientiously once we've handed responsibility for their lives back to our kids.

As far as those kids are concerned, shuffling the deck isn't an option. But everything else is on the table again: our partners, our work, our assets, the directions we want the rest of our lives to proceed in.

Few people toss out old clothes, relationships, or possessions without thinking about whether, with a little refurbishing, they'd still be useful. That goes for marriages, jobs, friendships, activities, habits, and attitudes, too. We build our new lives and new dreams on the foundations of our old ones. The dreams we've abandoned are replaced by new ones, based on the reality of what is still possible, the strength of our desire, and the wisdom to know that the journey is worthwhile even if the destination is never attained.

Holding up the dreams of the past to the mirror of the present provokes us to examine the question of what there was or is in our lives that we treasure and what is missing from them. The autonomy that comes with post-parenthood frees us to make new choices, and among the most important of these is the relationship we will have from now on with our grown kids.

Detachment, as we have seen, forces them to take charge of their own lives and frees us from the emotional responsibility for their choices. Autonomy allows us to freely choose the level of connectedness with them we want. Although we have separated from their problems, we rarely want to relinquish all other ties to them. And while that is largely up to them, it is our attitudes and behavior that will determine whether we can play the only role in their lives that is possible now: that of a friend.

A friend recognizes the limits of his responsibility for another person, even his child. A friend is realistic about another's strengths and weaknesses, even her child's. A friend sets and maintains appropriate boundaries in the relationship and defines the parameters of what he can and can't tolerate or condone and what he is and isn't able and willing to offer a friend, even a child. A friend respects the person, not her choices; if our respect is for the choices, it will come and go with every new choice our friend or child makes. A friend can balance the rival claims of his own needs and someone else's, even his child's. A friend forgives, especially her child.

Ideally, the parent-child relationship, which is inherently unequal, yields in our kids' adulthood—even their troubled adulthood—to a more mutual, peerlike connection, one maintained not out of need but choice. Even if they don't act like adults, unless we can see them that way the connection may be imperfect at best, unsustainable at worst.

As Judith Viorst writes, "Letting go of our vain expectations as parents and children, we learn to give thanks for even imperfect connections."[5] Laying down our burden of disappointment in our kids, we liberate them from it, too. And hoping only that our love will support them in their efforts—sometime, if not now—to get on with their lives and make the best of them, we get on with our own.

Notes

~

Introduction

1. Terri Apter, *The Myth of Maturity* (New York: W. W. Norton & Co., 2001), p. 23.
2. Ibid., p. 22.
3. Daniel Levinson, *The Seasons of a Woman's Life* (New York: Ballantine, 1996), p. 71.
4. Apter, *The Myth of Maturity*, p. 24.
5. Ibid., p. 226.
6. *National Household Survey on Drug Abuse*, U.S. Department of Health and Human Services, 2001.
7. William S. Aquilino, "The Returning Adult Child and Parental Experience at Midlife," in *The Parental Experience in Midlife*, eds. Carol D. Ryff and Marsha M. Seltzer (Chicago: University of Chicago Press, 1996), pp. 423–453.
8. National Institute of Child Health and Development, *National Survey of Families and Households*, 1994.
9. U.S. Department of Health and Human Services, Public Health Service, Centers for Disease Control and Prevention, Reproductive Health Information, Surveillance Report, 1998.

10. Carol D. Ryff, Hyun Lee Young, Marilyn J. Essex, and
    Pamela S. Schmutte, "My Children and Me: Midlife
    Evaluations of Grown Children and of Self," *Psychology
    and Aging*, Vol. 9, No. 2 (1994): 196.

Chapter One: The Kids Are All Right . . .

1. Michael Gross, *The More Things Change* (New York: Cliff
   Street Books, 2000), p. xiv.
2. Carol D. Ryff, Hyun Lee Young, Marilyn J. Essex, and
   Pamela S. Schmutte, "My Children and Me: Midlife
   Evaluations of Grown Children and of Self," *Psychology
   and Aging*, Vol. 9, No. 2 (1994): 200.
3. Ibid., p. 203.

Chapter Two: We're Waiting . . .

1. Terri Apter, *The Myth of Maturity* (New York: W. W.
   Norton & Co., 2001), p. 182.
2. Robert Bly, *The Sibling Society* (New York: Vintage Books,
   1996), p. 232.
3. S. C. Feinstein, "Identity and Adjustment Disorders of
   Adolescence," in *Comprehensive Textbook of Psychiatry*,
   4th ed., eds. H. I. Kaplan and B. J. Sadock (Baltimore:
   Williams and Williams, 1985), p. 1762.
4. Erik Erikson, "The Human Life Cycle," in *International
   Encyclopedia of the Social Sciences* (New York: Crowell,
   Collier and Macmillan Inc., 1968), pp. 286–292.
5. James Cote, *Arrested Adulthood: The Changing Nature of
   Maturity and Identity* (New York: New York University
   Press, 2000), pp. 1–3.
6. David Gutmann, *Reclaimed Powers: Men and Women in*

Later Life (Evanston, Ind.: Northwestern University Press, 1994), p. 7.

7. J. Bloom-Feshbach and S. Bloom-Feshback, eds., *The Psychology of Separation and Loss: Perspectives on Development, Life Transitions and Clinical Practice* (San Francisco: Jossey-Bass, 1987), pp. 160ff.

8. T. Benedek, "Parenthood as a Developmental Phase," *Journal of the American Psychoanalytic Association,* Vol. 7 (1959): 379–417.

9. Cote, *Arrested Adulthood,* pp. 166–169.

Chapter Three: Whose Fault Is It, Anyway?

1. Lara Adair, *Hold Me Close, Let Me Go* (New York: Broadway Books, 2002), p. 19.

2. Anne Roiphe, *Fruitful* (Boston: Houghton Mifflin, 1996), p. 228.

3. James Cote, *Arrested Adulthood: The Changing Nature of Maturity and Identity* (New York: New York University Press, 2000), pp. 95–98.

4. Thomas Bulfinch, *Cupid and Psyche and Other Fables* (New York: Modern Library, 1996), p. 49.

5. D. W. Winnicott, *Collected Papers* (New York: Basic Books, 1958), p. 223.

Chapter Four: They're Ba-a-a-ck!

1. Alexandra Robbins and Abby Wilner, *Quarterlife Crisis: The Unique Challenges of Life in Your Twenties* (New York: Tarcher/Putnam, 2001), p. 3.

2. Jeffrey Arnett, "Emerging Adulthood: A Theory of Development from the Late Teens through the Twenties," *American Psychologist,* Vol. 22 (2000): 469–480.

3. M. S. Mahler, "Symbiosis and Individuation: The Psychological Birth of the Human Infant," *Psychoanalytic Study of the Child,* Vol. 29 (1974): 89–106.
4. William S. Aquilino, "The Returning Adult Child and Parental Experience at Midlife," in *The Parental Experience in Midlife,* eds. Carol D. Ryff and Marsha M. Seltzer (Chicago: University of Chicago Press, 1996), p. 70.
5. Ibid.
6. Terri Apter, *The Myth of Maturity* (New York: W. W. Norton & Co., 2001), p. 28.
7. James Cote, *Arrested Adulthood: The Changing Nature of Maturity and Identity* (New York: New York University Press, 2000), p. 6.

Chapter Five: The Challenge of Independence

1. Alan Riding, "Italian Court Rules That Son Knows Best About Leaving Home," *The New York Times,* April 6, 2002.
2. Laurie Ashner and Mitch Meyerson, *When Parents Love Too Much* (New York: Avon, 1990), p. 39.
3. M. V. Bloom, *Adolescent-Parental Separation* (New York: Garner Press, 1980), p. 278.

Chapter Seven: The Limits of Love

1. Robert Lifton, 2002. Myownmind.com.
2. Mariana Caplan, *When Sons and Daughters Choose Alternative Lifestyles* (Prescott, Ariz.: Hohm Press, 1996), p. 98.
3. Ibid., p. 177.
4. Dwight Lee Wolter, *Forgiving Our Grown-up Children* (Cleveland, Ohio: Pilgrim Press, 1998), pp. 32–35.

Chapter Eight: Separating from Their Problems . . .

1. Jo Brans and Margaret Taylor Smith, *Mother, I Have Something to Tell You* (New York: Doubleday & Co, 1987), pp. 6–8.
2. Judith Viorst, *Imperfect Control: Our Lifelong Struggles with Power and Surrender* (New York: Simon & Schuster, 1998), p. 181.
3. Rachel Pruchno, Norah D. Peters, and Christopher Burant, "Child Life Events, Parent-Child Disagreements, and Parent Well-Being: Model Development and Testing," in *The Parental Experience in Midlife*, eds. Carol D. Ryff and Marsha M. Seltzer (Chicago: University of Chicago Press, 1996), pp. 561–607.
4. Ibid.
5. Brans and Smith, *Mother, I Have Something to Tell You*, p. 188.
6. William S. Aquilino, "The Returning Adult Child and Parental Experience at Midlife," in *The Parental Experience in Midlife*, eds. Carol D. Ryff and Marsha M. Seltzer (Chicago: University of Chicago Press, 1996), p. 448.

Chapter Nine: Reinventing Our Lives

1. Jo Brans and Margaret Taylor Smith, *Mother, I Have Something to Tell You* (New York: Doubleday & Co, 1987), p. 314.
2. David Gutmann, *Reclaimed Powers: Men and Women in Later Life* (Evanston, Ind.: Northwestern University Press, 1994), pp. 202–203.
3. Ibid.
4. Roger Gould, *Transformation: Growth and Change in Adult Life* (New York: Touchstone, 1978), pp. 217–226.
5. Judith Viorst, *Necessary Losses* (New York: Simon & Schuster, 1986), p. 261.

Bibliography

Adams, Jane. *I'm Still Your Mother.* New York: Delacorte, 1994.

Ashner, Laurie, and Mitch Myerson. *When Parents Love Too Much.* New York: Avon Books, 1990.

Bly, Robert. *The Sibling Society.* New York: Vintage Books, 1996.

Brans, Jo, and Margaret Taylor Smith. *Mother, I Have Something to Tell You.* New York: Doubleday & Co., 1987.

Bulfinch, Thomas. *Cupid and Psyche and Other Fables.* New York: Modern Library, 1996.

Caplan, Marina, M.D. *When Sons and Daughters Choose Alternative Lifestyles.* Prescott, Ariz.: Hohm Press, 1969.

Cote, James. Arrested Adulthood: *The Changing Nature of Maturity and Identity.* New York: New York University Press, 2000.

Erikson, Erik. *Selected Papers.* New York: W. W. Norton & Co., 1987.

Gould, Roger. *Transformations.* New York: Touchstone Press, 1978.

Gross, Michael. *The More Things Change.* New York: Cliff Street Books, 2000.

Jones, Landon. *Great Expectations.* New York: Ballantine Books, 1981.

Lasch, Christopher. *The Culture of Narcissism.* New York: W. W. Norton & Co., 1979.

Levinson, Daniel. *The Seasons of a Woman's Life.* New York: Ballantine, 1996.

Littwin, Susan. *The Postponed Generation.* New York: William F. Morrow, 1986.

Males, Mike. *Scapegoat Generation.* Monroe, Me.: Common Courage Press, 1996.

Robbins, Alexandra, and Abby Wilner. *Quarterlife Crisis: The Unique Challenges of Life in Your Twenties.* New York: Tarcher/Putnam, 2001.

Ryff, Carol D., and Marsha M. Seltzer, eds. *The Parental Experience in Midlife.* Chicago, Ill.: University of Chicago Press, 1996.

————, Hyun Lee Young, Marilyn J. Essex, and Pamela S. Schmutte. "My Children and Me: Midlife Evaluations of Grown Children and of Self." *Psychology and Aging,* Vol. 9, No. 2 (1994).

Schneider, Barbara, and David Stevenson. *The Ambitious Generation.* New Haven, Conn.: Yale University Press, 1999.

Stockman, Larry, N.D., and Cynthia Graves. *Adult Children Who Won't Grow Up.* Lincolnwood, Ill.: Contemporary Books, 1989.

Toder, Francine. *Your Kids Are Grown: Moving on With and Without Them.* Norwell, Mass.: Kluwer Academic Publishers, 1994.

Viorst, Judith. *Imperfect Control.* New York: Simon & Schuster, 1998.

————. *Necessary Losses.* New York: Simon & Schuster, 1986.

Wolter, Dwight Lee. *Forgiving Our Grownup Children.* Cleveland, Ohio: Pilgrim Press, 1998.

Index

About the Author

JANE ADAMS, PH.D., has been chronicling the lives of American families for over two decades, in ten books and numerous columns, articles, and essays. A graduate of Smith College, she has an M.A. and a Ph.D. in psychology. She completed psychodynamic training at the Seattle Institute of Psychoanalysis and has studied at the Washington (D.C.) Psychoanalytic Foundation. A founding editor of the *Seattle Weekly*, she has appeared on network radio and TV and lectures widely. She lives in New York and Seattle.